STAND UP AND FIGHT

Words of Courage from
a Women's Boxing Pioneer to
Unlock Your Faith and Conquer Fear

DALLAS MALLOY

Stand Up and Fight

Copyright © 2024 by Dallas Malloy

Scripture quotations taken from the Amplified® Bible (AMP)

Copyright © 2015 by The Lockman Foundation. Used by permission. lockman.org

ISBN (hardcover): 979-8-9905956-1-3
ISBN (softcover): 979-8-9905956-2-0
ISBN (e-pub): 979-8-9905956-0-6

Published by Lord & J.J. Press

For signed copies, bulk orders, or requests for interviews
and speaking engagements, email:

dallasmalloy@duck.com

https://dallasmalloy.com/

https://www.youtube.com/dallasmalloy

Cover design by Dallas Malloy

Editing by Margaret A. Harrell, https://margaretharrell.com

Photos for TERRIBLE, WILL YOU STAND UP? and SLAVES & CRIMINALS
by Dallas Malloy

Photo for FACES by Anette Puskas

Back cover photo by Josh Jacobs

Cartoons by Dallas Malloy

Dedicated to the God Most High,

To my beautiful Don,

And to all who fought and died for freedom,

those fighting now,

and those to come next.

ORIGINAL MUSIC
By Dallas Malloy

ORIGINAL SONGS - DOWNLOAD HERE:
(also available on Amazon and Spotify):

"TERRIBLE" - https://music.apple.com/us/album/terrible/1596428101?i=1596428102

"SLAVES & CRIMINALS" - https://music.apple.com/us/album/slaves-criminals/1602847282?i=1602847283

"WILL YOU STAND UP?" - https://music.apple.com/us/album/will-you-stand-up-single/1614868310

"FACES" - https://music.apple.com/us/album/faces-single/1633361994

"HE TRIED" - https://music.apple.com/us/album/he-tried-single/1641296663

ORIGINAL MUSIC VIDEOS:

-"Terrible" (Official Video) #donotcomply #nomandates #resistance #justunfriendmenow
https://youtu.be/xuv1U8A2svQ?si=2dFeCfiC2sainlYF

–"Slaves & Criminals" (Official Video)
https://youtu.be/LD912FrzlmM?si=-THnMrxNmuS0KRiJ

–"Will You Stand Up?" (Official Video)
https://youtu.be/BS2ArUwd3xQ?si=_iQTFL6loVnjSrP0

–"Faces": (Original Song)—video TBD
https://youtu.be/2_5osq-etx4?si=ARnu0OcLvB_aYgal

–"He Tried" (Official Video)
https://youtu.be/oar2JaqFc28?si=jM7pWoBqdU8vV5B9

A Light for God

Will you stand up and fight?
Let your vision ignite?

Stop dimming your light,
to receive God's sight?

Rise up not to incite,
but to do what is right?

Be the love you invite?
Refuse not to shine bright?

Will you be salt and light?
Let your spirit take flight?

With all of your might,
Will you stand up and fight?

—Dallas Malloy

Contents

AUTHOR'S NOTE

I was honored to be inducted into the 2023 International Women's Boxing Hall of Fame—a perfectly timed symbol for the necessity to stand up and fight. The "Night of the Stars" tenth-anniversary induction ceremony, a two-day event, took place in Las Vegas. I was in the midst of some of the finest champion boxers and coaches. The place was alive with passion. As I took pictures and signed autographs, I enjoyed the satisfaction that goes with it and appreciated a sense of vindication. But what struck me most was the authenticity and warmth among the attendees—the palpable respect among us. All had fought or coached—or loved someone who did. The boxers, though as varied as could be, had in common: a heart for boxing and the grit to have made enough of a dent to be acknowledged. That level of deep-down sincerity can't be faked; you reach it when forces fought you to not be who you are, but you went ahead anyway. It was, all in all, a glorious time.

The acknowledgment couldn't have been timelier. In this book—not for myself alone—I want to amplify the alarm bells sounding across the country and ricocheting through the globe. Now, more than ever, telling us: *this* is a time to stand up and fight.

When I was fifteen and started boxing, I was told *no.* *"Female boxers shall not . . . compete,"* the USA Boxing Rulebook stated plainly. I pursued and won a discrimination lawsuit for the right to box and became the first female in the United States to have a sanctioned amateur fight against another female. And won by unanimous decision.

I stood up then because it was right. The obstacle in my way was unjust and needed to be taken down in order to follow my dream. I had to fight just to get into the ring. And I didn't fight for women's sports to be demolished. Now more than ever the relevance of that returns. We need to stand up and fight.

I watch a deteriorating culture steadily demean and devalue female athletes—which is wicked enough in itself—but is only a fragment of the obvious attempt to gut this country from the inside out and obliterate most of what is good. **This is not what I fought for.**

I witness people being coerced and bullied by a loud, weaponized minority. Much worse, it is *allowed* by the apathetic and uninformed, the cowardly hiding in corners, and the evil bent on destruction.

I see mental oblivion and total disregard for those who fought for our freedom in the United States while those of us with open eyes battle daily to keep this unique and remarkable nation alive. The ingratitude is a disgrace. And I get it; I was a dumb kid once too. But I grew up. And I *never* hated my country. The hypnotized and dopamine-addicted cling to their one-dimensional reality, doomscrolling for their next hit of outrage and terror. This, they do without introspection. The constant craving sponsored by technology is quite a thing to manage, and witnessing the devastating effects, I'm not sure how many of us are up to the task. While this has all been biblically prophesied, it is still surreal to watch good portrayed as evil, and evil as good.

I see this as the last round, and there is danger in letting our fatigue blind us from the fact that we are winning. It is a time calling for great courage. There is no such luxury as remaining neutral. Pretending evil doesn't exist isn't fighting it; **it's promoting it.**

This is the time to build muscle made only in trenches, to be refined and perfected. We have to press on, no matter if in the midst of hate and attack. We may be persecuted, but we won't be forsaken. Be bold and courageous and stand up to deception. **Don't comply with a lie.**

People tend to shrink from giants, but fearlessly running toward them is how your wings appear. Pray for courage. May God bless you, and I will see some of you in the trenches.

PART 1

RIPPING DOWN

So many friends turned out to be enemies. Like waking up from a dream realizing you're actually deep in the wilderness, I trudged through the thorny, painful, illuminating recent years of life training. But the light of hope was ever present and, with steady focus, has strangely grown brighter. The muscular structure of endurance takes time to build and is always worth it, though it rarely feels so during the burning-away process. The hyper-condensed experience of loss, breaking, and awakening is not for the weak. It is an opportunity to shed all you thought you were—to wake up into a new, bright existence, elevated in seeing and being. *But first comes the ripping down.*

Maybe from experiencing the insidiousness of addiction, I spot enemies quickly, whether inside or out. The liars of the mainstream media were no match for the chatterbox of the alcoholic mind working around the clock—both with the same goal: to deceive, distract, and destroy. They remain unsuccessful—**praise God.**

Early in 2020, I knew things weren't what they seemed to be. One unmistakable giveaway was the level of desperation from the alleged experts to *sell*, the blatant psychological tactics, the coercion, bullying, and famous gaslighting. The melodramatic slogans intended to scare and pacify were stupid on their face. *"Alone together."* Yeah, that doesn't actually work. And no, I will not *"stay safe."* I will, however, **stay free.**

To be clear, I know the steady, orchestrated attempt to dismantle this country has been going on for a hundred years or more, and although I never held any real trust in the overreaching institutions, this is what it took to fully wake me up. I spent plenty of time in life being deceived; I was still swimming in the blue Kool-Aid I grew up drinking. It took this ripping down to reveal the conditioning for what it was, and the shameful realizations followed. I loathe the carnage in its wake, but that's what it took for me. *I repent.*

I'm grateful for the painful revelations. As with so many others, our eyes have opened up in horror and remorse to the lies we were fed, growing up. Revealed for the sham they are, old ideas and conditioning have been burned off in healing fires and replaced with the cool, refreshing light of truth. The awakening is ongoing, as more continues to be uncovered.

This was only made possible by everything tipping so radically, demanding attention and deep investigation. The power of willingness, discernment, and critical thinking allowed for real, deliberate, thoughtful change. Euphemisms I grew up with that I used to repeat freely, a flood of truth had washed away, revealing the ugly reality of what was rotting underneath. I can understand the unwillingness to look. No one likes to be wrong, but

I started to see the light shining through and needed to know the rest.

The lie *"we all want the same things"* stood exposed for what it is: denial that evil exists, thus promoting more of it with this seemingly benign statement, either out of ignorance or craftiness.

It is possible to think wrong things without being a coward, but it takes courage to admit you've been wrong, and even more to make right any damage done. Intelligence allows for a change of mind. And the heart, where God also works, can be transformed with a willingness to be shown. Then the rebuilding can happen.

As many succumbed to psychological warfare, a great divide emerged. In 2020, a friend went from saying, "The thought of a 'vaccine' coming out so fast *'scares me'"*— cut to 2021—to saying: *"I'll be the first in line."* The only difference was who sat in the White House and about a year of being pummeled nonstop with military-grade propaganda had passed.

Scared stupid went to a level I'd never witnessed on such a large scale. Watching grown adults so excited to show their compliance—*I'm good! I'm good! I'm not like those **other** people. I'm not like those germ spreaders!* Doesn't this sound familiar? *Herd mentality.* It reminded me of a five-year-old excitedly showing their finger-painting skills, desperate for approval. Not so cute on an adult. But many ate it up. They even got stickers to proudly display their obedience. So cringe.

The celebrities gleefully promoting the denial of emergency healthcare to the unjabbed was quite a spectacle.

Shamelessly wicked in their completely deluded state, their attitude was: if one of those nasty anti-vaxxers dies of a heart attack while the jabbed are placed ahead, *oh well, they got what they deserved.* In true masturbatory style, they celebrated their made-up superiority while their equally mindless followers clapped along with all the idiocy they dished out (and continue to).

These are the types of people who "went along" during the Holocaust, the brutal regimes of Stalin, Pol Pot, and all murderous tyrants throughout history—and, sadly but unsurprisingly, right now. Different names and faces, but that is all. Being the easily fooled cowards that they are, they cave, not seeing themselves. Status, titles, and degrees are irrelevant. If the injustice is happening to the "other," they look the other way; they are the ones who pretend not to see, only stepping in when it costs them nothing—yet offers a virtue signal, sure to impress their brainless counterparts. They were the ones who wanted conservatives/the unjabbed/questioning (*thinking*) to be fined, imprisoned, put in camps, "re-educated"—just think of how extreme that is—and worse, pathetically justified the position by their brand of ever-changing pseudoscience. Without critical thinking, they crave the approval of the unreflecting herd, and, needless to say, are without honor. Short of a major life-shaking spiritual transformation, they will not change. Never trust them.

Criticizing so freely isn't my usual style, but these are the ones who wished us *death* because we didn't fall for the gag. Their ludicrous attempts at peer pressure failed miserably, making them all the more enraged, not because they have the compassion they laughably claim, but each doubt shed more light on the absolute lie of their cult religion. To my view, they surely would have turned a blind eye if you were thrown into an oven. The comparison didn't escape me.

They wanted us punished for *thinking*. They are the crowd without humor or the ability to connect the simplest of dots. They are without self-reflection. They are the dumb followers of the day. **We will never forget.**

In this strangely condensed period of time there was tremendous grief and anger with the loss of jobs, opportunities, daily familiar faces, and so-called normal life. Acting and other production work was mostly reserved for those who obeyed. Many film sets were segregated by jab status. You don't believe me? *Yes, they really were.* But losing in rapid succession what I thought were friends and family to the mainstream-media mind virus, I found especially chilling and surreal. I learned early in life to suspect that people were basically weak and dangerous, but this shredded any remaining doubt.

Already grieving personally (my marriage had been slowly breaking and finally shattered at the end of 2019), I had been in a heart state that left the mind wondering how much longer I had to endure this realm. As with all grief, coming in agonizing yet manageable waves, it made sense that 2020 initially put me in a brief, emotionless shock. Living in Los Angeles, where it's a constant shakedown at every turn and trouble jumping out of the sidewalks, it was a peaceful jolt to prepare for the storm of awakening. Always living in head-on-a-swivel survival mode takes a toll. Insane policies and people are daily reminders you are unwelcome. So a blow to the norm was an unusual and refreshing reprieve before the hits to come. We all have to go to the corner in between rounds. But only for a minute.

Within three years that same marriage was fully *restored*. An unexpected gift—from the fire of oblivion came a new creation after God broke off what needed to be gone, rebuilding the good. But that's a lovely miracle I cherish, to tell about another time.

Along with the heartache and crushing of any leftover naïveté about human nature, more was stripped away. It was a time of necessary ripping down and shedding all that wasn't useful. It was good to be awakened to what I had thought was a semi-trustworthy system, plainly showing itself to be anything but and, with each red pill, acknowledge how silly that was. *I repent.*

At some point in 2021, I was given symphony tickets to hear Beethoven. Being one of my greatest loves, this was a special treat. Alas, being happily jab-free—*verboten!* I can't fathom telling the wide-eyed six-year-old me that just started the glorious journey of piano study I would later be deprived of the exalting experience of live music for not participating in a medical experiment. Are we awake yet?

By the end of that long second year—measuring from "two weeks to stop the spread" (d'oh!)—everything had shifted. I was sharpened like a blade and grateful for the divine fire that has continued to burn and reveal. I realized when you are willing to die for the truth, you are separated and changed. And free.

I observe those who are still the same—living in self-made bubbles with blinders on (and usually face diapers)—and

I feel a loss on my side they can't understand. They don't comprehend the severity of what they condoned. And they either don't care or don't realize how they threw so many of us under the bus. Others know *exactly* what they did, but the temptation of a sense of superiority, however phony, was too delicious to pass up. Do they not have any empathy or integrity? And if so, where are they hiding it?

As I write, we see a greater push to lean in even further to total horror. Witnessing the brutality of terrorist attacks in Israel was nothing less than terrifying. But also sickening and impossible to comprehend are those proudly celebrating these acts of war, including instances where there are protesters in the West who take the position that some victims are deserving of rape, death by fire, and other atrocities merely because of where they live, or for not checking enough boxes on the intersectionality scale. Can you comprehend this?

Because they see Palestine as oppressed, and since the Jews are White, they're OK with them being terrorized and tortured. Stop and think about that. Do you think you can settle differences with such a mindset? There is no middle ground there. *No, we do not all want the same things.*

A flank of political figures act as though Israel shouldn't be able to defend itself. Of course, there is antisemitism among many of them. Intersectionality theory focuses on power based on group identity, so if you're Caucasian and male and heterosexual, you're perceived as having the most power and, therefore, can't be discriminated against—in other words, if someone was attacked by an anti-White racist, it couldn't be labeled racism. Do I really have to point out how savage this is? How dangerous? Even setting aside the shameless hate-driven double standard, do you see the false premise of this "thinking" reducing us to race and nothing else?

Based in deception, intersectionality theory promotes the lie that we are not individuals and is, categorically, trash: dehumanizing. It pushes group identity—such as race, gender and sexuality—above all other considerations in determining our worth, degrading individuals down to specific traits and demographics factors. None of this has to be verified, by the way; if you just *declare* you belong to a part of a particular group that makes you more valuable within the system, it must be accepted without question. But I'm sure no one would dream of taking advantage of that!

It is irrelevant, anyway, because while some luxuriate in playing the game of *top victim*, it's still based on the lie that we are not entirely *unique* beings. Nevertheless, as with any narrative, if you get rewarded for falling in line, and it is repeated enough, a large portion will believe it. And too bad if it looks like an opportunity to profit at the expense of others. That's totally OK if you've been convinced not only that those *other people* deserve it, but furthermore—they *owe* you.

I think it's fair to say that those in this frame of mind are *sick*, don't want peace, and are incapable of love. Having completely bought into collectivism, they have zero compassion or acknowledgment of the immeasurable number of variables that make each human intricately, marvelously unique. Tragically, I suspect, some are on board due only to their absolute ignorance—therefore are susceptible to what they are being told is *brave*, in that way making up for a devastating lack of purpose. Vulnerable to powerful persuaders and manipulators, they go along with those who seek to ruin and remake humanity in their own image. Lacking all regard for the individual, they are successfully brainwashed into dehumanizing all who don't accept their cult. A lack of knowledge is destroying them, and the reckoning for these contemptible perpetrators will certainly come.

Courage is vital to face down such evil taking place. And it takes courage to stand. The beautiful thing is, the more you do, the easier it gets; it becomes a part of you. It can sometimes feel like an eternity of standing is required before the tide turns. But even if everything seems against you, it doesn't matter because the standing in itself changes you for the better and eventually becomes who you *are*.

Are *you* the one who stands when no one else will?

Are *you* the one who doesn't cave?

Are *you* the one who is unshakable?

Endurance is the muscle that builds from the refusal to stop forward motion within the pain and discomfort of conflict.

As a little kid in Washington (state), I didn't feel courageous when I was bullied in school, but I guess I was for *enduring*. I internalized so much of it, not knowing a better way to get through. Having courage to *go through* things isn't comfortable, but necessary. It is the *going through* that effects change and expansion. And after-the-fact comes the reward of the muscle formed only by enduring. Already paid for, it can't be snatched away, now built into your very being: an unbreakable framework—constructed, piece by painful piece, with steadfast, patient endurance.

Spiritual armor is the failsafe, the ultimate, the incorruptible, the unshakable. I wasn't shown that part available to me and only discovered later, when sought through pain by necessity.

Sometimes the arrows are coming from every angle at once, and there are those you can't see until you realize you're bleeding to death. When I made boxing history at sixteen years old, it was just **barely**. Many forces were trying hard to take me down at the time. An abusive relationship was steadily chipping away at my soul, degrading the already limited sense of self I had, fostering a monster of shame and irreconcilable internal conflict. The beginning stages of alcoholism had its hooks in me but had been kept at bay by an all-consuming focus on boxing. This cruel romance finally set it on fire, contributing in a variety of ways to my near self-destruction. Depression loomed, and bulimia fueled the chaos.

Persisting in spite of myself, I kept my laser focus on training. The passion and inspiration that drove me to eat, sleep, and breathe boxing, continued to light the way for my vision, and I won the historic fight handily. But soon after, the afflictions took over one by one. Adversity and betrayal accelerated their progress, and I was swallowed up into a time of darkness. Eventually, God helped me crush those enemies beneath my feet.

I shattered them so that they were not able to rise;
They fell [wounded] under my feet.
For You have encircled me with strength for the battle;
You have subdued under me those who rose up
against me.
—*Psalm 18:38–39*

Sitting in rehab at nineteen years old during the initial intake, I noticed on the wall a framed picture of a sandy beach. I could see words written down the center. Unable to focus on anything the counselor was saying, somehow in my broken-down state, I was able to look a little closer and read what I realized was a poem titled "Footprints in the Sand." I had never heard of it and didn't know where it was going. I was shaken when I read the last line. It conveyed something I'd never dared to dream. The word *wow* shot through my drug-poisoned mind, and a moment of light pierced through the slowly deteriorating wall of angry defiance. My heart was momentarily gripped by a love I hadn't known existed. There was more to be torn down, and I wasn't done researching yet. But a pinprick of light was a beginning.

It is easy to hide from spiritual things with philosophical pontification and over-intellectualizing, but these mental traps only obscure the light of truth behind manmade complexity. They are not the tiniest bit spiritually productive or forward moving. Addiction has a nice way of sweeping all that aside, producing a peak state of reasonable desperation, where finally the healing light of God can pour in, shining on you fully.

In order to become something worthy and great, many things need to be broken off. When I finally got sober and my eyes were opened to the spiritual side of things I dared not see before, I knew there was no going back. Not to blindness. It is the *dread* that creates pain, and resistance prolongs it. With all growth, there is inevitable discomfort, but avoidance causes even more suffering. Tears unshed hurt more than their release.

A broken time is for cleansing and purifying. I have found spiritual things will have their way with or without my participation. But with my cooperation, a whole world of great possibility is unleashed; joy can enter, along with an unexpected serenity, regardless of circumstances.

Diving headfirst into the paradox of surrender defies rational thought, but it is in that place I have had all spiritual revelation that altered the course of my life, and always for the good. Coming to the end of yourself seems at first like a bitter, desperate conclusion but is actually a moment near perfection, opening the way for a new beginning.

I left boxing as a heartsick, broken teenager and could easily have lamented what was taken from me, but there's no victory in that. I'm proud of what I accomplished, and grateful for the unforgettable times, memories and powerful lessons gleaned from intense high-level training. More came from a few years of hyper-focus, discipline, and the insatiable willingness to learn, than might have been derived from decades of half-hearted effort. It further developed the same principles of devotion and discipline I'd started learning as a six-year-old, studying piano, and continued evolving in weight training and eventually bodybuilding competition and acting.

The burden of a big vision and many talents is the limitation of time—preventing you from taking everything as far as you want to take it. With spiritual direction, I have learned to keep *experience greed* in check, know where to put my focus and when it's time to move to the next mission.

Be unshakable and unbreakable.

I had to be broken more than once for the deep healing and building to happen. This tough schooling ultimately made the ripping down of 2020 and beyond not only bearable, but productive. Like Michelangelo chiseling away all that was not *David* in order to find him, it is more about uncovering and actualizing the creation already there.

It is worth the tribulation to become unshakable and unbreakable. Why waste time floundering in doubt and uncertainty? A brilliant life awaits at an energy state far higher than what the world teaches, with its ruthless and miserable, mind-numbing negativity. Like gravity, it is always working to pull you down. This isn't a picture of the abundant life available to us.

In recovery I learned the paradox of *surrendering to win.* I received that revelation down in my being, where it could be *lived,* not just bandied about for some useless philosophy talk. Not that everyone has to go through addiction; anything that brings you to your knees will do, and from that place, make a way for this awakening.

Don't fear the ripping down in order to create something new. Time in the wilderness is worth the refining fire. It is always harder before it gets easier. But like a broken bone, it regrows stronger and denser through the pain of healing, given the proper nourishment.

Will you stay standing?

Each morning I am fresh clay awaiting the Master Sculptor to direct and mold. When I am pliable NOT to the world but to the Creator, it is *good*.

My people are destroyed for lack of knowledge . . .

—from Hosea 4:6

We are pressured in every way [hedged in], but not crushed; perplexed [unsure of finding a way out], but not driven to despair; hunted down and persecuted, but not deserted [to stand alone]; struck down, but never destroyed;

—2 Corinthians 4:8–9

For you have need of patient endurance [to bear up under difficult circumstances without compromising], so that when you have carried out the will of God, you may receive and enjoy to the full what is promised.

—Hebrews 10:36

PART 2

THE CURRENT THING

When I was boxing, I had some great supporters in my corner, but pioneers always take arrows in the back. Without fail, not complying with "the current thing" ignites fear-based opposition.

At sixteen, I got a crash course in having my words twisted. Not only was I misrepresented, but being interviewed, I was asked things like, "Why would a pretty girl like you want to box?" That came from a female interviewer. Of course, I didn't think I was pretty, but I knew it was a stupid question. Did she think I was vain and didn't want my face hit with a boxing glove? No doubt. It never crossed my mind. Besides, a black eye was a badge of honor.

A producer for one of the late shows asked if I could come tell a story about breaking a nail during training. Break what nail? I was a boxer. I didn't have "nails." And if you need more—a *piano virtuoso*. What pianist has nails? You'd think that would be interesting enough, but he wanted cute. It wasn't cute, and I didn't want to play the game. I didn't do the show. It might sound idiotic to you—and it *was*—as other interviewees who were asked similar questions will tell you. But believe it or not, that's how it was at the time. Everything changes. Sometimes for the better, sometimes for the worse. Usually both.

On fight night, I entered the ring with the American flag draped across my back. But even that provoked some criticism. I was celebrating both pride and gratitude for being in this great country that allowed me to fight clear-cut discrimination and win. After that, it became a common practice for athletes to wear their country flag.

Loved and remembered

To live on a higher energy level requires willingness to be set free from the shackles of the *current thing*. I know this isn't for most people. Most will fall in with the crowd and go along. But you are not part of the most. Are you? You are set apart. Aren't you? You know it. All you have to do is accept it and live it fully. You already have the tools you need, or they will be provided at the right moment in time, as happened to me.

When I started boxing, I saw a show about a young girl training to be a doctor. Her father advised her that sometimes patients in their little village would be unable to pay but that she should help them anyway. He said *money is nothing; to be loved and remembered is everything.*

It sounds sweet and unrealistic now—and it is. God knows money is a necessity. But the meaning is what stuck with me; the deeper drive and motivation to rise each day—that was the heart of it.

What are you living for?

How do you want to be remembered?

Who do you see when you look in the mirror? Who do you want to see?

The last few years have been especially silly and stupid in regard to the *current thing*. Sometimes it has to get radically stupid for people to take notice. When the lockdowns started in 2020 and the attempt to force things upside down went into overdrive, I hated to watch so many swallowed up by lies. But the loss and betrayal of glazed-over friends and family was no match for the necessity to stand up for facts and logic. Looking back with no regret is priceless. It is well worth the cost of being unliked and ridiculed by those zombified by propaganda. While it is sad to toss a life preserver to a sinking fool who refuses to take it, I pray for their awakening and will never stop speaking the truth.

It's time to **be encouraged**. The aim of this book is to help unearth the strength, power, and courage at your disposal. This is the perfect time. Watching many people shrink down behind shadows to fulfill the world's low expectations, I am fed up. You've already guessed that. Unaware of the power at their fingertips, those ensnared by psychological warfare toss aside their unique gifts out of fear or just to belong. You can't be comfortable *and* stand up to the mediocrity mob. I'd actually love to be comfortable. Surprised? It would be much easier, I'm *sure*—but living in such a state of denial and betraying myself and others is unthinkable. Once again, the dream of doing nothing slips through my fingers like water.

There has never been a more essential time to stand. Every time you do, the muscle of courage builds and grows. The alternative is to live a scared little life. To close your eyes and hope it all magically goes away, as if you don't have a great and incomparable assigned part to fulfill, is no existence at all.

As surreal as it is to have to say this, men shouldn't be allowed in women's sports. Duh. On the surface it's outrageous and laughable, but watching this disaster play out is witnessing a crime unfold. The motives behind it are sinister, and out in the open for all who choose to see. The loud minority arguing for this have most likely *never played a sport in their life*, making an already-insane "argument" even more worthless, if that's possible. For many following along, it's just fulfilling a pathetic need to be relevant at any cost. Either way, it's a cruel joke on women and girls, with potentially fatal results. But it's worth it to not be called a bigot, right?

As a boxer, I sparred with men. But it would have been ludicrous to have to compete against them, for reasons which used to be considered common sense: testosterone levels, muscle mass, bone density, size, reach, speed, lung capacity . . . need I go on?

What happens to a girl who knows she's no longer honored as the female she was perfectly designed to be? Being robbed of the chance for fair competition and potentially life-changing opportunities and livelihoods, being forced to "compete" against biological males and share bathrooms and locker rooms, are vile methods to swiftly crush, even disintegrate, hope and ambition. What an effective way to break a spirit while simultaneously shaming her just for being a girl. As if that weren't enough, allowing potential male predators into women's prisons is an example of the most bizarre enslavement imaginable. These overt attempts at female and male erasure are always backed by a constant bombardment of bullying and gaslighting to manipulate the public into going along. Of *course* they are—if these were tenable ideas, they wouldn't *have* to be forced. No matter how loud it gets, don't buy them. Ideas so twisted were satire material until this wretched agenda was allowed to infiltrate and infect the mainstream.

And there is no demand for logical consistency; one pushed idea is that gender isn't real; another is that you can become the other gender. Both can't be true. It's funny how contradictory that is, if you feel like laughing. But there is no accountability: whatever narrative is convenient and fits a particular situation is supposed to be accepted blindly, or shame on you. All of this serves to further hypnotize and degrade the sleeping and the frightened, ever reminding the awake that it's in our nature, as people, as a whole, to easily be swayed. But many more continue to awaken every day.

These almost impressively crazy ideologies have taken hold solely because many have stood by and done nothing. This opened a way for those aggressively pushing their dismantling scheme on a distracted public. Anyone semi-intelligent or better knows this is a total fail, only worthy of laughter. Nevertheless, to those genuinely caught up in these ideas, it is very concerning. Never allow yourself to be silenced by an irrational fringe with a loud voice.

The *current thing* hits people where it hurts: the desire to be accepted. It prods and tempts us to *go along*, and as a general rule, the herd hates those who don't.

The current thing has never been my guide. I'm often struck by the lightning rod of inspiration through an external sign or vessel—which serves primarily as a catalyst to spark an inner directness already taking place. That is, whether I understand it or not, the dominating force of inspiration pulls me along. Even when I didn't have the emotional development to match my vision, I had to follow it. There is a price, but it's worth it. I like a challenge and get bored with the mundane and the ordinary.

I'm *certain* it would be easier to blend in, but I've never been able to ignore the inspirational spark. As a kid I never did and was often made fun of and teased, sometimes ignored and sometimes respected. But it is all the same. If you are like the timeless character George Costanza (*Seinfeld*), where *everybody has to like me!* life is an uncontrollable crazy-making prison. The remarkable Dr. Wayne Dyer used to talk about becoming *independent of the good opinion of others.* It's not easy to learn, but it spells **freedom**.

When I was boxing, nothing about it was the *current thing*, so I took heat for it. But strong drive and passion always trump my desire for comfort and acceptance. I've never gotten flack for being a pianist, but to me it has many of the same elements as boxing: drive, inspiration, and discipline.

Being an actor is generally accepted—it's entertaining but rarely taken seriously. Bodybuilding has never been the current thing; it's mostly unaccepted but by a few who worship it. Some respect it; others are confused or disgusted by it. But it's all so irrelevant; what part of any of this will matter in a year? Inspiration will always override the current thing.

Standing up to shadows

Do you see how the fear that tries to keep people from speaking up is a lie? Most of the adversaries are illusions. The primary battlefield is in our minds. When you stand, enemies appear. But allies will also. That power far outshines the haters and the trolls. There's a reason people self-destruct when their life is consumed by hate—it's one of the most damaging energy states. I'm not a Pollyanna, by any means, but I know good prevails. Though we live in a fallen world, good outlasts evil. When you stand up for truth, it may take a long time for others to see—and some never will—but truth is still truth. Those who tend to follow along are likely to be vicious when you stand up. I think it's best to expect them to and focus mainly on the ones who are with you. But keep an eye on the other.

Do you need permission to be free?

Do you need permission to be great?

This is your hour to stand and fight. *Are you standing? Fighting?* Do you put on your spiritual armor and go into battle: at work, at home, in conversation? Don't let the masquerade go by; don't let yourself be manipulated and kowtow to the agreed-upon lies. **You are never alone in this**. Call out the corruption wherever it appears and crush this mass lesson in peer pressure. Free yourself from the wretchedness of people-pleasing and codependency.

The current culture has completely confused *enabling* with *love*. Humoring delusion and mental illness whether out of ignorance or cowardice, is in reality, hateful. Tolerating a destructive relationship isn't love. Being browbeaten into believing you have to *go along* with the absurd or be labeled a bigot isn't love (or sanity). True love and compassion *don't endorse your annihilation.* But it takes courage to call it out. The truth may offend, but that doesn't make it any less true. Boundaryless compassion always ends up causing harm. Anyone with children knows this unless they're raising insufferable brats, soon to be society's problem. Enabling requires no backbone, only a tolerance (condoning) of evil. No guts.

You know it takes discipline to do what is right, and it is not always popular. The same principle applies on a national scale. Right now we are watching a total disaster play out at our wide open borders. It's clear this invasion is by design, not a lack of discipline—no borders means no country. They don't have to conceal what is undeniably malicious intent. At any level, the catastrophic result of *no borders no boundaries* is essentially the same: pure chaos, and bad for all. It is *compassionless* and shows weakness. And weakness breeds aggression.

It can be a chore to go against the current pushed narrative, but it's necessary when it is a lie. The mediocre-minded crowd always fears the unusual and the fantastic. Just imagine where the world would be if it had shut visionaries and inventors out. My vision, like their vision, as it happens, is always ahead of the current thing.

What if you really leaned into God?

I've been pushed to the edge until there was nothing to do but rise up and be better. In the darkest of the last few years I began leaning into God without reservation, like never before. All of my worldly hesitation and doubt fell away because there was nowhere else to turn. The distraction of analysis became irrelevant; I saw it wasn't the answer. And for me there had to be a decision: whether I am living for the world or for God. It can't be both. Living for the current thing is living for the world. I used to want the approval of people, but human nature is clear; the first chance it got, if I didn't fall in line with the groupthink *de jour*, this mad crowd would just as soon leave me bleeding in a ditch. The lowest nature will always be fearful and selfish, excited to *other* some group to boost themselves. Only dazzling in their own eyes and maybe their fellow sheeple, they too will inevitably turn and devour one another.

I invite you to jump in headfirst; to be loved and remembered. Not by the world system, but by God and the love of God in others' hearts that remains when all the nonsense and self-obsession are swept away. You are already loved by God anyway, dear heart.

Stand up to deceivers. Beware of the appeal to authority as proof of anything. Don't comply with a lie. God gave you discernment to use.

Standing up doesn't have to be pretty. It just has to be done. When I started bodybuilding, I learned the German phrase *Ich muss perfekt sein—I must be perfect*—at the time, fully embracing addictive perfectionism. I did workaholism to intensity until the inevitable burnout schooled me in *diminishing returns* and the harm that ripples out from there. Perfection is a fool's goal, doesn't work or impress, and burns excess energy for no good. You don't have to stand up perfectly. It doesn't even have to be done without fear. *You just have to do it.*

People drag themselves around with difficulty, wearing a heavy cloak of pain, shame, and a thousand fears. I see it. Afraid of their own potential and confused by the darkness, they obsess . . .

What will people think?

What will they do?

What will they say?

Will I get the clicks and likes?

Refusing to be mentally brought down by one-dimensional thinking and others' judgments will build a storehouse of unshakable power. Darkness cannot survive in the presence of light; a single flame destroys it. Realizing this life was never about the opinions of others, but between God and me, has concentrated my focus and continues to break away any remaining fear or concern.

Many go through life afraid to look at their potential, wearing their failures as self-protection from greater things, replaying the losses and guaranteeing their story stays the same. A culture championing victim status makes it all too easy. Of course, they're actually cheering your demise, cannibalizing their own cult members to satisfy an endless hunger that will never be fulfilled this way. Never once have I encountered a successful on every level person that had a victim mentality. They are all *overcomers*. I know there are people who have made a living out of playing the victim—maybe even a great living—but I don't view them as truly successful. No matter their financial worth on paper, they still carry the heavy disempowering pain of a victim mind and can never reach anywhere near their full potential. They can never be *free*, in heart and mind, and at peace. Locked in that mindset, they are forever dependent on others providing constant proof of their victim status. And if it doesn't exist, they manifest it. We've all seen this—when the demand is greater than the supply—cue the latest racism hoax. Our minds will create whatever we are fixated on, particularly when it validates an identity. In order to maintain their personal narrative, they are doomed to remain broken.

Of course, racism exists, but the reality is nothing like what the lamestream media aggressively spews—pretending White supremacy is a serious current threat while simultaneously pushing anti-White racism. The media *loves* racism—as long as it's directed toward the chosen target of the day. It's easy enough to see this is total garbage when you step away from the screen and interact with the third-dimensional people. There is nothing secret about this method, attempting to keep us angry and divided. Don't fall for it.

Are you a people-pleaser?

A world-pleaser?

A God-pleaser?

The danger of the current thing

Sometimes the current thing is your own thinking. It can be the greatest threat; keeping you in procrastination and dread, and cemented into a comfortable, deconditioned rut in body and mind. *Are you ready to break from the downward pull of the inward current thing?* Or maybe you already have but need the encouragement you aren't getting from those around you or even yourself. Here it is:

Each new day is an unpromised experience and chance to start over. Even this single moment can be a focal point for a new start if the day is too much to grasp. *Any fraction of time unfolding* holds new possibility. Did you notice that word "fraction"? We make the mistake of carrying emotions into the next moment and the next. Sticky and addictive, they seem hard to shake off.

Practice not being a slave to emotion by **setting your mind** on the right actions and **keeping it set.** You *will* make progress. Sometimes we have to *act* our way into *right thinking.* To dictate the next action, people too often make the mistake of relying on their ever-fluctuating feelings: "I'll do _____ *when* I feel motivated." I promise you it will never come, and even if it does, it won't be sustainable.

I'll start working out **tomorrow.**

I'll eat healthier **tomorrow.**

I'll drink more water **tomorrow.**

I'll start praying and meditating **tomorrow.**

I'm too busy.

I can't afford it.

I don't have time.

Tomorrow never comes.

I've trained a thousand people without a gym or equipment.

No one is busier than me, and one minute of something is still *something.* Zero will stay at *zero.* The principle of

momentum guarantees if you only *start and keep going*, even if at a snail's pace, **you will** *move forward*. And inevitably, things will open up for more if you don't quit and trust the process.

Everything costs *something*—time, energy, resources. Being unfit physically, mentally, and spiritually extracts a terrible cost. To you and all those around you. Even though the bill doesn't necessarily arrive until later, it's immeasurably cheaper to invest your time, energy, and resources *now*, breaking through the rut and caring for yourself on all levels.

Take right action, and the desire to do it will follow. People have always said to me: *I wish I had your discipline; I wish I had your talent, etc.* Everything is wrong with this. For starters—these are just excuses.

Wishing accomplishes nothing.

Talent carries a large, ongoing responsibility. It's a thing of beauty to those on the outside, but it's actually a work order. It is not an end, but a *beginning* to something potentially great if utilized with dedication and persistence. It's an endless marathon, not a trophy.

And I have no magic potion called *discipline*. When I want to get something done, I just make deliberate decisions, maintain a laser focus, take the necessary steps to get there, and work through obstacles when they arise. I *persevere*. It has nothing to do with how I *feel*. Being inspired is glorious, but I can't force it or control if and when it happens. **Action, focus, and follow-through** are everything. Passion is essential but can't be the only ingredient. Believe me, hours of tedious scales on the piano don't feel super inspirational. Months of intense training in a caloric deficit, preparing for competition, also does not feel amazing. Sixteen hours on a film set, doing multiple takes while mentally fried, is anything but glamorous. I thrive on these complex challenges, and that fuels the discipline that makes it possible. But discipline is still a decision. Emotions lie and shift constantly; they can't be the driver.

Most importantly, I've learned through many trials to make no move without consulting the Helper. It is a practice: the better I get at *listening*, the better I get at *hearing* and *receiving* Assistance.

The current thing in the world system is never to *love*, but always and forever to break and hate, divide and conquer. In a million fantastic forms, there is nothing new. When I remember the love God placed in my heart that moved me as a child to marvel at the fact that there are no two of us exactly the same, never to have existed before and never to again, I see the soul of each person. And then from the eyes, shining through the layers of pain and frustration, sadness, mistakes, hurt, and anger, there is the light of God. Imagine, you haven't even begun to see the greatest things of which you are capable.

Set your mind and keep focused habitually on the things above [the heavenly things], not on things that are on the earth [which have only temporal value].

—Colossians 3:2

And do not be conformed to this world but be transformed and progressively changed by the renewing of your mind . . .

—from Romans 12:2

The Light shines on in the darkness, and the darkness did not understand it or overpower it or appropriate it or absorb it [and is unreceptive to it].

—John 1:5

Put on the full armor of God [for His precepts are like the splendid armor of a heavily-armed soldier], so that you may be able to [successfully] stand up against all the schemes and the strategies and the deceits of the devil.

For our struggle is not against flesh and blood [contending only with physical opponents], but against the rulers, against the powers, against the world forces of this [present] darkness, against the spiritual forces of wickedness in the heavenly (supernatural) places.

Therefore, put on the complete armor of God, so that you will be able to [successfully] resist and stand your ground in the evil day [of danger], and having done everything [that the crisis demands], to stand firm [in your place, fully prepared, immovable, victorious].

—Ephesians 6:11-13

PART 3

REBUILDING

Weight training and boxing taught me to turn weakness into strength by—beyond everything else—focusing on the weak points until they transformed into strong points. Doing the opposite of what the flesh wants always brings a reward—such as the empowerment experienced from training hard and pushing the perceived limits. Muscle is broken down and regrown *better, stronger, faster.* Like the productive pain from the work to build muscle, there is always, with new growth, a sting and burn. But the reward is so sweet you are willing to do it again and again. Because all development works this way, don't shy away from it. Create opportunities to train spiritual musculature and run *toward* the giants. Don't delay your victory until it's too late and you are demoralized by cowardly indecision. Don't wait to be devoured by self-loathing; instead, eliminate the dread with precise and deliberate action. *Praying for courage is one of the most effective weapons available.* Will you do this?

After surviving the ripping down of what I'd thought was reality and normalcy, I was able to wake up in a red-pilled state of clarity; *clearer, sharper, stronger.* As I learned to rebuild with the right tools, everything became more meaningful and time was condensed. A lover of efficiency, I grew even more focused and selective about energy spent. I learned in recovery to reach for God, but somehow that lesson needs to be refreshed daily, sometimes every minute. The last few years brought that to light—now it's my *first* choice, instead of reaching only in moments of desperation, then going about my day when the crisis is over. There is an anonymous saying: "*When the storm has passed, God is forgotten.*" I learned the hard way to *pray without ceasing.* How many crises have been averted or dissolved before they could even start by taking this preventive measure? More than I can know.

The path of recovery, humbling at every turn, is a great and treacherous adventure. At two years sober, it was time to face down another opponent: smoking. For this, I had to go to a higher level. Cigarettes and coffee were splendid in the early days, but to get fit again, I had to leave behind a two-and-a-half-pack-a-day habit I both worshipped and hated.

With weight training and basic cardio, I returned to where I'd started before boxing. Running a couple blocks' worth on the country road back in the sticks where I lived in Oklahoma ended with wheezing and coughing the first few times. But it got better. This was all part of the stop-smoking plan, which I attempted multiple times during those early days back at training.

I joined a gym and started at the bottom like in high school—one or two plates on the weight machine, small dumbbells, and a bar. I had regressed terribly. I didn't care, knowing if I was *steadfast,* and just made a *start,* even with baby weights, I would build up better and stronger. At the gym I picked the stairs for cardio for the same reason the machine was usually free; it's the hardest one. I started with ten minutes before coughing forced me to stop and catch my breath.

Every moment of struggle helped to further build a recovery foundation. Brick by brick. On my sixth attempt, I broke things off with cigarettes. It was the *worst;* like having the skin ripped from the body, my soul writhed as I slogged through days of torment to finally arrive at the relief and freedom on the other side. One thought carried me through those first days: *This will definitely pass, and I don't want to be a smoker forever, so if I just don't light up, I will never have to go through THIS again.*

A couple years before that, as a thin, lost, alcoholic addict, I drove about twenty-four hours straight from California to Oklahoma, arriving in one piece only by grace. Seven years later when I left, I was sober, strong, and lean. Forty-five minutes going all out on the stair machine after an hour of hard weight training was my usual. But to get to that point, I started with a vision and wheezing on a country road. Only by God's strength was this transformation possible.

I stand up and fight against the adversary within by choosing to follow God's guidance to the best of my ability. Again and again and again. It isn't about my personal will power, except for the proper use of it—to align it with the Divine. I fight with that most potent decision, in every moment choosing Power over my own force.

When I was prompted to move back to California and start a new chapter of rebuilding, the first days back were anxiety filled. In Oklahoma, I'd left an ex who owed me a small fortune—the last of the master manipulators. More accurately, the last of my codependent foolishness. But it was one of the toughest things I had to do. Besides, departing the special place where I'd gotten sober seven years before was risky and caused me great sorrow. But I was compelled, insistently and persistently, and though I tried to ignore it at first, I *had* to go. Guidance fueled my focus into deliberate action. I had to put my heart on ice just to be able to leave so many loved ones and that beautiful flat land.

I have definitely learned that if I'm being prompted in a way that is *consistent, insistent, persistent, and good*, it's probably God. My most important task is listening and discernment, and trust.

Arriving back, just me and my beloved cat, Yuki, I continued working out and took schooling to earn my first personal training certification. Soon I started competitive bodybuilding. There is no more accurate, raw example of breaking down and rebuilding than this. The strategic training process encapsulates a *wilderness season* perfectly; a time of testing. Breaking down for the purpose of refining and perfecting. To be a living statue was the goal.

Outsiders to bodybuilding often see it as narcissistic and shallow. But the drive for me was the constant, unrelenting challenge to be better, grow, build, and create. When focus becomes so sharpened that one perfect repetition at a time becomes *everything*—in order to be better for the next and the next—it magnifies living in the present, to an extreme degree. Far beyond the thrill and satisfaction of the physical exertion, what stands out are the changes in the mental structure; they bring the lasting effects and rewards.

After my first competition I'd been through a battle. I came back to the gym, feeling changed. In many ways, the competing process is a self-imposed prison, with its regimented schedule and protracted blocks of extreme requirements and restrictions. But a few moments of near physical perfection on stage—after months and years of sacrifice—solidify and affirm the decision to go all in with your entire being. They are the sublime moments that perfectly symbolize the benefits of following through, which remain long after competition day. Each time, high levels of confidence were setting in, as well as the ability to maintain extreme focus and endure as long as necessary for a specified goal.

All of this first came with the ripping down of the basic desire to be comfortable, food-satisfied, and in a cozy, energy-reserving state. Then I could be rebuilt. Building muscle can't be done without breaking down and rebuilding new, or without pain and sacrifice. If physical rebuilding requires pain and breaking, of course the same goes for emotional and mental growth and healing. Don't fear the burn of rebuilding to **become greater**.

As with anything taken to an extreme, there are many pitfalls. I see now where bodybuilding absolutely became an idol. Thank God, that was worked out of me. And gratefully, as the detrimental aspects of it were shaken off, even after I stopped competing, what was valuable remained.

Everyone says the film business is tough, but I'm tougher.

About the same time, I started getting jobs as an actor. Offering some of the best training imaginable, theater helped me move rapidly into film and TV. In this industry, breaking and rebuilding is constant, both as an actor and in navigating a nonsensical business environment. Fortunately, I've been trained to deal in the abstract. Intense schooling as an athlete carried over, along with further improvement in the realm of acting: learning to be comfortable being uncomfortable, managing delayed gratification or none at all, being steadfast and patient, keeping my eye on a vision—and by all means, not taking things personally. Otherwise, your heart will be so damaged it is unlikely to recover. Without the embodiment of these lessons, instead of breaking down for the better like shedding ego and self-consciousness, it would be easy to fall into emotional *breakdown.* But how likely is that to occur in Hollywood? I mean *really . . .*

In those days, I still fixed everything with a hammer. My modus operandi was harshness and force. *God, please help me fulfill MY will.* But life was teaching me that some problems require a feather, not a hammer. A yoga teacher in high school had tried to instruct me in that, to help me balance out the powerlifting and weight training I was doing: clenching his fist he said, *if you walk around like this, you exhaust yourself. But if you walk around calm and cool, you're ready if you need to make a fist.* He planted the seed, but more time and tears had to be poured on before it grew into anything.

I used to make my own way in everything before I learned to call on God for help and knowledge of *His* Will—*in everything*. After many worldly defeats were painfully and wonderfully transformed into spiritual successes, that winning method solidified into my foundation.

I learned early to set my mind and keep it set on a thing—a piece of music to master, a script, a sport. Being naturally obsessive is an asset or a burden, depending on my aim. Everything sparked by passion, I ultimately achieved with grim determination when the inspiration ran low. *It just had to be done.* I later learned to offer up my desires to God for transformation and manifestation—trimming the fat of complaints, self-pity, and procrastination. Nothing is wasted then; and God can use me for *something sweet* and create a new thing far beyond what I imagined. Then I can step into the indescribable, and the peace which surpasses all understanding. The lesson of setting your mind and keeping it set still holds—but the focal point is **greater**. Instead of my own exhaustive effort, the energy comes paradoxically from a place of *rest*.

Rebuilding new habits and always refining, I learned to do the task I am dreading *first;* otherwise, *it* is the master. Dread, like any other form of fear, always falls apart when faced head on. Once this discipline becomes habit, it is a sharpened tool at your disposal and becomes easier and more automatic to reach for. *Do the dreaded task first.*

Rebuilding my outlook, I discovered both the ability and necessity to take spiritual authority instead of being mastered by emotions, liars that they are. A previous employer of mine was of the used-car-salesman variety:

shady and condescending. He incessantly micromanaged the staff and talked out of both sides of his mouth—which we all plainly saw. Morale was dismal. He used every angle and shortcut—including violating multiple labor laws—to cut corners and not compensate us. Naturally, I dreaded dealing with him and was thrilled to quit that job for greener pastures. But before that delicious moment came, I had to wait for prompting. There are times it seems God leaves us in difficult or even awful situations, but instead of playing victim (useless, pointless, false), I've learned to pray for what I need to glean from a situation so I can move through it as quickly as possible: *Please show me the lesson and give me the strength to endure while completing this course. Thank you!* In the meantime . . . I'll just have to sweat it out.

Driving to a staff meeting one day, I was anticipating confrontation with the boss man and started feeling the dread. Always a tragic waste of time, those meetings should have been condensed into a five-minute phone call or email. As I prayed for clarity, a new affirmation came to me. Strongly compelled to speak it aloud, I said: "I'm not *afraid* of confrontation. I *love* confrontation, *because it's a game.* And it's a game called *I WIN.*" I kept repeating it, yelling it. Of course, shouting while navigating Los Angeles streets was quite normal, but this was different. Immediately my energy shifted, and I became excited to get there. I couldn't wait. With renewed energy, I kept repeating the words. At the meeting I felt light and relaxed, taking from it what was useful and discarding the rest (most of it). The boss didn't mess with me that day. Maybe I was shining in a way that repelled him. But it didn't matter because I was armed with clarity; calm and empowered. Dread was reframed—transformed—into *strength*.

Another lesson in reframing came from an instructor in the film industry, talking about how to combat nerves while auditioning. Instead of trying to control them and calm the adrenalin, he said, just *use* it and think: *I'm excited! I'm excited about this opportunity to show my work and talent.* Then it becomes fuel, and fear becomes eager anticipation. I've used this many times when performing in acting and music, competing, and public speaking.

I remember an audition experience when I ran into a fellow cast mate from a play we'd worked on together. He told me about a stage performance he just did, where he had to run down the aisle, but halfway down he tripped and went flying. We shared a big laugh. Just then they called me in for the audition. I bounded in, enthusiastic, friendly, open, and smiling. Having laughed my nerves out, I nailed the audition without trying. Contacting me later, the director told me they gave the role to someone else but loved what I did so much they wrote in a role for me.

That time the energy shift came naturally, without having to deliberately reframe my mood—the gift of a belly laugh. But the experience was the same, and an indispensable lesson to keep.

Everything can be used for good. When Hollywood went along with all the quarantine and mandate madness, it just inspired more creativity. *Shut us out? No problem.* I became *more* inventive, *more* innovative, and *more* creative in making my own projects. Using everything for good is another way to stand up and fight. **No one can stop that.**

As a heartbroken teen, I would talk myself into getting out of bed, saying: "I'm OK, I'm OK." I didn't know to reach for God. After desperate attempts at prayer as a child that seemed to fail, I dismissed God and cast aspersions on those who believed in Him. An understandable response from someone hurting and lost. Thinking of God as a mystical bellboy, my misguided prayers seemed to cause more harm than good. Not getting what I wanted in the way I wanted it, I fell right into the predictable trap: blaming God and turning my back on Him, while the enemy laughed with glee.

It would be easier in the moment to go through life, seeking fix after fix, but *easy* isn't a worthy goal and only compounds pain and discontent. *Easy* won't fulfill or create anything great or memorable. The desire to carry out something beyond this world builds a tower of fearless resilience. Knowing this life is **bigger than me** brings freedom and purpose. The endless supply of distracting, addictive substances and activities is clearly the work of spiritual wickedness in high places. Do you see the effort to pacify the population with these methods? Yuval Noah Harari, advisor to the WEF (World Economic Forum) is quoted saying: "What do we need humans for? Or at least what do we need *so many* humans for? At present, the best guess we have is keep them happy with drugs and computer games." A tad creepy, no?

The World Economic Forum is an organization best known for its push for "the great reset" and drive for global governance. In 2016, founder Klaus Schwaub put out a video of a dystopian vision for 2030, stating: "You'll own nothing and you'll be happy." Sounds kinda spirit-breaking to me.

Larry Flint, CEO of BlackRock, the largest money-management firm in the world, and WEF contributor said, "You have to force behavior." Do you think it's appropriate to shove down woke policies on companies?

I'm not a fan of having a small group of self-appointed officials dictating how the world should live. Just the unbridled arrogance of telling the plebs *how things are going to be* should raise red flags. Calling attention to their nefarious statements may earn you a conspiracy-theorist label. That is so tired. And lazy. I suppose at this point it's a badge for weathering the war on information. Please dig deeper. Always beware of those seeking to control what you can do and what information you can see.

How do you feel about a tiny group of elites deciding what's best for you and your family? Do you think they should tell you what car you can drive or whether or not you can own property? We didn't vote for these people. They don't have to hide because many still don't want to see. So they continue to say the quiet part out loud, and work to force down behavior until enough people have had enough.

That's a funny question: "What do we need humans for?" Hey, what do we need *globalists* for?

People are free to numb themselves, but it will never fill the hole in the soul. And no amount of drugs or games can ever compare to even a sliver of a reflection of spiritual awakening. Noisy, unelected figures can continue attempting to play God, but that doesn't give them real authority. No matter how big these "giants" believe they are . . . they ain't.

I didn't really understand spiritual warfare until the last few years, when I became willing to look and learn. It's tempting to get dragged down with culture-war issues. But the real battle is in the spiritual realm. I will continue to fight here, as directed, but spiritual tools are the primary weapon. We don't wrestle against flesh and blood. In the past I would have thought this was dumb and crazy. But many true things are often called dumb and crazy before you are ready to hear them.

In part, God used music to rebuild me. At five days sober, I was driving down an Oklahoma highway in my Chrysler New Yorker with a crooked front end, crumpled from a final night of boozing. "Heaven Beside You" came on the radio, melting my hard exterior as only music can do. I suddenly knew I had to play piano again. I had swiftly tossed it aside, along with about all else that I loved, at a pace only addiction can pull off; it takes everything smooth away before you realize it's gone. The words *God help me, I want to live* went through my mind. I glanced to the right as an RV was passing by just then with one word on the side: BRAVE.

As much as my self-destructive behaviors had tried, I was grateful for their failure and couldn't deny in that moment: it took more guts to *be here* than trying to leave. I accepted the challenge to really live, without reluctance.

Recovery is a continual experience of being humbled, broken, reshaped and rebuilt. So is living for God. An absence of this process results in a soft, silly, aimless society—in which it's so easy to stand for nothing and fall for everything. I guess that's what happens when you've never been punched in the face.

Happiness is a stupid goal

... and it's a relief to be free from pursuing it. That freedom creates ease and acceptance, which ends up fostering more and more moments of that ever-fleeting thing: happiness. I didn't say it's bad to be happy; but making a *feeling* a goal is a setup for failure—why chase a moving target?

Worthy goals are *meaning and purpose, strength, and personal progress.* Meaning and purpose inspire motivation, energy and resilience, bringing the experience of happiness. When strength is earned, whether physical, mental or emotional, it is deeply rewarding. It opens doors, helps those who witness, and builds confidence. Making personal progress is necessary in everything. Endless work without results is torment. Performing fulfilling work can definitely be part of the reward, but there has to be forward movement. Being strong and making progress make people happy.

I've always been compelled forward to create, break ground and continually get better. So I haven't grappled with a sense of lacking purpose, but like a knife pressed to my side, I've always known a constant drive, discontent, and pressure. Untamed, that drive can go as bad as it can go well—and drive me right into the ground. Inspiration is often the fire that lights everything up and opens the creative pathways. But if I'm out of alignment with God, my solo mind is compelled to pour on the gasoline to speed things up and do it *my* way. All of my research using this method ultimately produced imbalance, addiction, and strife. Test complete: no more experimentation required.

When I do everything to serve God, I live in a *calm delight* that comes from joy. That doesn't mean feeling fantastic all the time; it is an ongoing practice that takes discipline. *But so worthwhile.* Keeping my focus on God, praying always for His Guidance, through both the smooth times *and* the extended trials, I can have incredible peace and power. It relieves me from the burden of perpetual emptiness that invariably comes from a self-focused life. We were not made to be self-serving; narcissism inevitably breeds misery. If you are unsure of your own purpose, meaning will *always* be found in prayer and finding ways to be of service.

Show me who I can help today. Show me what You want me to do today.

Challenge: help someone without being found out and without telling anyone. (No selfies.)

God shines in our weakness.

God broke me to build me—better and stronger. If I'm rebuilding with my own will, the foundation is weak. If I accept guidance from the Counselor, it is good and strong. God shines in our weakness and uses tools and forms unique to the heart of each person. I have been led in ways only I would recognize, understand, and appreciate.

Each weakness is an **opportunity** for increasing strength and growth,

Each weakness is an **opportunity** for greatness,

Each weakness is an **opportunity** to shine.

Out of the divine fire came a new creation—
unshakable, unbreakable —
nothing missing, nothing broken.

This nation is broken but *not ruined.* We are not, by any means, finished. And we can rebuild it. It requires the individual's *decision* to *stand up and fight*, unite, and refuse to be bullied and conned. The insanity ends when people say they've had enough and, most importantly, start *living* that they've had enough. When on all levels we refuse to live beneath our ability—to be sharpened and refined—we can rebuild from the inside out in order to stand taller as individuals. And as a nation will become greater than ever before. Believe it is possible, declare it, and do it.

And we know that God causes all things to work together for good for those who love God . . .

—from Romans 8:28

. . . [My] power is being perfected in [your] weakness.

—from 2 Corinthians 12:9

Be unceasing and persistent in prayer;

—1 Thessalonians 5:17

And the peace of God [that peace which reassures the heart, that peace] which transcends all understanding, [that peace which] stands guard over your hearts and your minds in Christ Jesus [is yours].

—Philippians 4:7

For our struggle is not against flesh and blood [contending only with physical opponents], but against the rulers, against the powers, against the world forces of this [present] darkness, against the spiritual forces of wickedness in the heavenly (supernatural) places.

—*Ephesians 6:12*

Whatever you do [whatever your task may be], work from the soul [that is, put in your very best effort], as [something done] for the Lord and not for men.

—*Colossians 3:23*

PART 4

WAR SONGS
MORE WAYS I FIGHT

W*hy would you get a tattoo on your face?*

We are in a war . . . have you noticed? Who asks a superficial question during a war?

It says: **Defend Freedom**. It is a declaration and commitment—permanent war paint that will never stop being necessary, relevant, and true.

I discovered Tom MacDonald's music in early 2021. He's a fearless and brilliant chart-topping rapper/singer in spite of being fully independent. He is frequently called "controversial" because he criticizes wokeness and says true things. The nerve! His words made me feel free. Becoming more aware of the persistent methods the culture had been using to chip away at us, I realized how I'd been suffocating. Waking up to the dulling effects of my early conditioning, I was **grateful** it was being broken out of me.

I've been composing music since childhood, mainly for the piano—often while sitting in class in high school. I had started to do more songwriting by this time, and for about a year was training as a singer—since I really needed more to do, right? But I realized rap was the perfect medium, combining my love for poetry, purpose, and efficiency. The ability to convey so much so fast came naturally and helped to solve my continual scramble to keep up with the flow of ideas. Plus it's so damn fun.

TERRIBLE

Lyrics for the first song I released in 2021, "Terrible," were initially sparked by one sad and completely unnecessary situation in particular, in which I was ostracized at a place where I was a longtime volunteer, taking care of cats and kittens. Some of the management revealed themselves to be complete covidiot nazis. There was a moment when one of them came around, hassling us to wear the compliance cover (mask). Another manager said it was OK not to. But the dictator stated, referring to me, *"Well, we have to wear it around **you** anyway because . . ."* She couldn't even finish the sentence. Because *what*? There was still at least a small part of her that knew it wasn't right. But she had collapsed into the unrelenting narrative, and knowing I hadn't harpooned myself, she went along with the bizarre lie that taking an experimental injection made you a magical non-spreader (and a good person). *And also, everyone else had to get it in order for it to work.* Huh? Oh, yeah, that makes perfect sense.

Some agreed with me but kept silent for the most part. It was heartless, stupid, and entirely non-science-based.

After a couple more incidents like that, I'd had enough. Thank God I had emotionally prepared to leave for a while because I'd known for several months it was time to move on from there. But I knew how hard it would be to not see my kitty friends, so I'd been dragging my feet. I went for one final visit and for the first time they asked me: *Are you vaccinated? (show me your papers). Well, we can't let you in.* They singled me out, just looking for a reason; apparently they didn't approve of the Let's Go Brandon shirt I wore the time I'd gone before. Grubby jeans and t-shirts were the standard there, but suddenly after eleven years they had a dress code—for me. I bet everything if it had been anti-Trump garb, I would have been hero of the day. That's the cult for ya. Humorless and charm-free. I'm certain the cats weren't concerned with my attire.

The lesson: listen to God's persistent promptings and cooperate, or He will do what you can't do for yourself, which sometimes causes more pain. I just couldn't let go before that. I don't care for anti-human sentiment, but in this case it is easy to understand, based on their treatment of me and several others.

One of the managers called me later and apologized. But it was already past time to move forward, so that was the end point. I will always hold dear the countless treasured memories I have from there. Those golden times remain as they were.

I had just discovered Canadian clinical psychologist Dr. Jordan Peterson. His *GQ* interview from 2018 caught my eye late one night. Having to get up early, I hadn't intended to watch the entire hour and forty-two-minute interview, but I couldn't stop. Instantly respecting his fearlessness, brilliance, and precision of speech, I knew this was important, and he was someone to learn a great deal from. Among many topics, he discussed the danger of identity politics. I went down the rabbit hole to find out more about this formidable force. His disarming honesty and refusal to cave to the woke moralists—in spite of prolonged, intense hyper-scrutiny and persecution—impressed me. How extraordinary.

To me, it seemed apparent that most would rather be wrong in a group than right alone. I was becoming more aware of the *transgressive garbage* being pushed in schools and institutions. In new ways every day, the stupidity of it was breathing down our necks. Attempts to rewrite history, make your gender a choice, and erase Caucasian people, pretending we aren't still the majority in this country—to gaslight, control, and degrade—continue to fail. They're bound to. Have you noticed—thought about—the way the media is hell-bent on pretending we barely exist? The message is: *we want you to be the minority right now, or not exist at all. ALSO—oppressing you for your skin color isn't racism.* They can't have it both ways. This vicious and blatantly racist treatment would never go for anyone else. We've been overly tolerant, and it's time to STOP. Stop falling for the emotional blackmail. Racist, manipulative terms like "white fragility" and "whiteness." The message is loud and clear—*you better be quiet, don't have an emotion, don't be human, don't speak up, you are invalid.* Are you going to take that? Is that right or fair for *any* group? It seems the effort to tranquilize and torment has gotten to a small portion of us, and a larger portion ignores and plays pretend. With all the rest, it has unleashed a lion that will never stop rising up and crushing our unworthy opponent.

Lyrics from my first single "Terrible"—released 11/22/21:

TERRIBLE

I'm tired of your disrespect
You ostracize me thinkin' that is correct
Shame on you for believin' that's the answer
When all you do is parrot mainstream chatter
Try usin' that chemical bag up on your shoulders
Maybe then we wouldn't have to become soldiers
You make me your enemy and that's a tragedy
You forgot I stood beside you in calamity
Never mind, you hypocrite, I shake my head
In your blindness probably wishin' that I was dead
But that's how sick and crazy you've become
The powers got you now, nice and numb.

Terrible . . . terrible thing
Can't believe it's come to this
Terrible . . . terrible thing
Open your eyes, recognize, don't succumb to this.

I'll survive with a blade and a dream
I'm not the one hiding from the unseen
You've taken the easy way and don't even know
Most would rather be wrong in a group than right alone

It's fine 'cuz I don't need your permission
We were friends once but you made your decision
You got caught in the game by not thinking
Swallowed all their good poison without blinking
Thought you'd sleep your way through for a while
Ghost the rest and Pollyanna in style
But your house of cards will fall right on schedule
When the truth comes out—the bad and the dreadful.

Terrible . . . terrible thing
Can't believe it's come to this
Terrible . . . terrible thing
Open your eyes, recognize, don't succumb to this.

I'm tired of your disrespect
Take your CRT—all lies that you project
You've become what you hate and don't even see
You're a slave to the agenda of greed
You think you're smart and strong but you're just distracted
Won't care or even notice until you're subtracted
Wake and see you're wastin' your whole life
Bein' nothin' but a fake and makin' strife
Make up phony terms and labels to divide
But your straw men don't impress—we know you lied
You invent your own shame and bathe in the blame
Make your whole world insane, it's false just the same.

Terrible . . . terrible thing
Can't believe it's come to this
Terrible . . . terrible thing
Open your eyes, recognize, don't succumb to this.

You lie to yourself, it's a hard thing to watch
You know not what you do, you're just frightened and lost
You're goin' in circles so weak you don't fight this
So high on the group tellin' you that you righteous
Can't say it more plain
You're a maker of pain
Hypnotized and mundane
Brainwashed by the inane
Instigator, hater
Reality delegator
Sheeple, karen, manipulator
Propaganda regurgitator
You're sick on division, bad intention, cult affliction, mock religion
Scared stupid, forgot that you're human
Don't believe in the truth, live in delusion
Take your fake compassion virtue signal narcissism racist evil
I don't need it, I'll be here with the real people.

You live to play the victim and think you're off the hook
But your brand of suffering ain't the only one, you just fail to look
Shun me, run from me, fear me, that is all bearable
But the world will hear me, and one day . . . things won't be terrible.

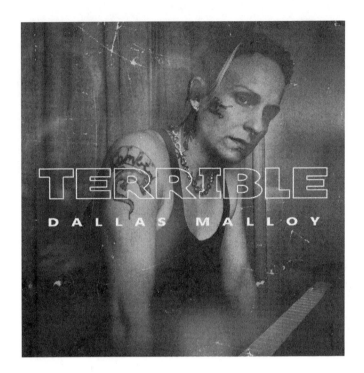

SLAVES & CRIMINALS

The next song came later in 2021, when a couple friends were talking about getting fake jab cards in order to work. I drove an hour out of my way and pleaded with them not to do it. We *had* to take a stand. Another acquaintance tried justifying it to me, saying *"I need to make money."* Unlike me? Unlike everyone? It was incredible. *We all need money.* We also need dignity and self-respect.

Don't misunderstand, I had considered it too in a shameful fleeting moment of desperation. But again, that's the idea, right? Isn't that the goal? To drive you to the point of being consumed by fear and willing to hand over your rights and freedoms? And what would be taken from you next? And next? One little compromise here, another there . . . then you're in quicksand, realizing you gave it all up and sold out all the people who fought and died for what you had. No way. That doesn't sound very American to me.

I told my friends that by going along with this, they'd be *perpetuating* this unconstitutional, authoritarian power grab. If everyone refused, we would shut it down. Granted the powers that (allegedly) be will continue trying to enslave us in more and more ways, but *we the people* have the authority. And have to keep standing and fighting.

But I have to travel. They won't let me. I have to pay my rent. I get it.

I told them to think it through. Getting the cards, they would be condemning themselves to lie—and to stay liars. If you do this, forget standing up or speaking out online or anywhere else. From then on, this will be how you go through life. It will mark you. Not to mention screwing the rest of us in the process. And what happens if they start checking them thoroughly? What then? Arrest? Prison?

No good could come from this, and I couldn't let them off the hook for being so terribly shortsighted. When the bugle sounded, what did you do? **And what about next time?**

I said to them: we can't let them turn us into slaves and criminals. This is how they want you—scared and controllable, disempowered, quivering in your boots, willing to do whatever they say for someone else to come fix it. I drove home and wrote "Slaves & Criminals," released 1/1/22.

SLAVES & CRIMINALS

You keep changin' the goal post tryna make us look guilty
Use your smoke and mirrors to mystify but we won't be bullied
Your fabrication, lies, manipulation, take your tyranny
You underrate our strength and power, it is very clear to me
The weak just get weaker but the strong we get stronger
No one is listenin' from this side any longer
We see right through you lies, agenda, propaganda machine
Keep your bad ideas and polarizin' far away from me
You keep tryna take a hold but it won't work we stayin' bold
Your overreach, coercion, gaslight tactics gettin' old
Your threats, intimidation and attempts at segregation
Only make us more aligned our power growin' 'cross the nation
You don't get to change us, we are standing together
Bully all you want, we love our freedom forever
Tryna traumatize and ruin our lives 'til there's nothin' to save
But you don't petrify with your lies you forgot we the strong
and the brave.

We will not be your slaves and criminals
We will not be your trash to throw out
We will not be your slaves and criminals
We the people, are not afraid to throw down.
You underestimate us
You will not degrade us
Your impact will be minimal
We will not be your slaves and criminals.

You might a thought I was done but there is so much more to say

You not the boss of me, you will not take our lives away

You wanna make things hard for us, tryna wear us down

But your bluff is weak—I see the twisted grin behind the frown

It is so creepy, why you so sleepy? you not gonna cheat me, you won't beat me

It gettin' too freaky, I wanna be weepy, instead I just scream I am free! I'm not dreamin'

This is a joke, you goin' for broke, thinkin' that we don't know, watchin' you choke

Tryna divide us and break down our souls until we explode but we won't—hell no!

You hate us, wanna trade us for information before you waste us

Thinkin' that we so useless you wanna shame us and tame us and blame us

But we're not a bunch of complainers or takers or makers of strange reputations

We're not arrangers of danger, enragers, forsakers, or fakes who mandate devastation

We the people that work, live, breathe, and create, the ones that make everything go

We the heartbeat of the world, the lifeblood, the pearl, the body, the spirit, the soul

We the ones still imagining hope, the ones connected to all living things

We the ones inspired to grow, it is our passion for freedom we bring.

We will not be your slaves and criminals
We will not be your trash to throw out
We will not be your slaves and criminals
We the people, are not afraid to throw down.
You underestimate us
You will not degrade us
Your impact will be minimal
We will not be your slaves and criminals.

We will never stop I hope you are listening
Enrage us all you want but remember this one thing
Together we are strong, we don't need your prescription
For a prisoner's life, we don't meet the description
There is something inside that you will never tame
A power you can't put your finger on or even name
Sharpened like a blade we just get better every day
An unstoppable force risin' up to stake our claim.

We will not be your slaves and criminals
We will not be your trash to throw out
We will not be your slaves and criminals
We the people, are not afraid to throw down.
You underestimate us
You will not degrade us
Your impact will be minimal
We will not be your slaves and criminals.

I'm happy to say my friends never went through with the cards.

WILL YOU STAND UP?

Every day was a battle then. (Not over.) The level of emotion all around was particularly heightened as we contended with a constant stream of gaslighting, enraging attacks on women's sports, anti-White racism, and our freedoms being threatened and stolen. (Also not over, and intensifying.) Each day is still about navigating which crisis needs my attention first. *These are dark times*, a friend reminded me. *So it's no wonder my soul is churning.*

About a month or so after "Slaves & Criminals," continuing to be shamed by the puppets in charge and eating the red pills like candy, I was listening to an interview with scientist and physician Dr. Robert Malone. He spoke about mass psychosis, awakening, solutions and hope. He mentioned the necessity for *integrity, community, and dignity*.

There were moments then where hope seemed dead, and I sensed the hearts breaking all around me. The pressing call to action and flickers of the remaining good poured into lyrics and melody. On 3/22/22 I released "Will You Stand Up?"

WILL YOU STAND UP?

Will you stand up? Or will you stand by?
Will you speak facts and call out the lies?
As it falls apart, will you shut your eyes?
Will you feel proud when you realize?
Will you wake up before your demise?
Will you stand up? Let me summarize:

Will you stand by and let women become third class citizens?
Let her sports get ruined pretend you don't see the difference?
Labeled victim or oppressor either way's a sentence
Bullied into false beliefs makin' your skin a prison
Cancel those who don't agree, destroy their life and image
Say it's all OK so you don't have to make decisions.

The only way outta this findin' a common thread
Listen to this one thing if nothin' else I said

Finds its way in your heart keep these few things in mind
Stop for a minute remember a different time

Other things mattered . . . lives . . . dreams
It wasn't so them and us . . . no . . . a little bit . . . integrity
Hope still existed . . . more . . . community
Yeah, that is the answer
Oh . . . and dignity . . . yeah . . . division's a cancer
No way to run a society . . . we all need redemption
We the ones who make it possible, time for reinvention
This is your turn now, do not comply.

Will you stand up? Or will you stand by?
Will you speak facts and call out the lies?
As it falls apart will you shut your eyes?
Will you feel proud when you realize?
Will you wake up before your demise?
Will you stand up? Let me summarize:

Will you stand by and let others' rights be trampled?
Look away as we are segregated and dismantled?
Give up on your freedom 'cuz you took it for granted?
Call it all conspiracy 'cuz you can't imagine?
See all through a lens of race creating more damage?
Try erasing all the men like that's an advantage . . . damn.

Maybe you think it's too late but it's not
That's the problem when you give up power of thought
It's all up to you now and this is your time
Reimagine that hope and step up to the line

Other things mattered . . . lives . . . dreams
It wasn't so them and us . . . no . . . a little bit . . . integrity
Hope still existed . . . more . . . community
Yeah, that is the answer
Oh . . . and dignity . . . yeah . . . division's a cancer
No way to run a society . . . we all need redemption
We the ones who make it possible, time for reinvention
This is your turn now, do not comply.

Be fearless today . . . or there's nothing left
If we can't speak the truth that is our death
Time to be brave now . . . stand up . . . for what is right
You can't just wait around . . . for someone else to fight.

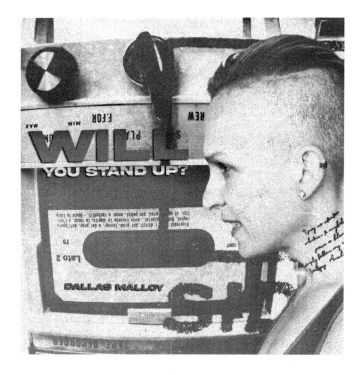

FACES

I wrote "Faces" earlier in 2021, before I gave up trying to reason with the clueless. The other songs were coming to me strong, so I didn't release it until 7/6/22. The predictable results of a soft society creating problems in order to find meaning is so tiresome and disheartening. Covering faces, such a great way to dehumanize and sow division. And super helpful for rioters—I mean protestors—(not really)—to hide their identity while throwing public tantrums and wreaking havoc on innocent civilians. Making life generally worse for all. Funny how they always seem to wear masks while outside. "Fiery but mostly peaceful," of course. Cowards.

Having to stare at diaper faces on a daily basis, witnessing the unraveling culture and the nauseating virtue-signaling circus, spurred most of this track:

FACES

I see the mass psychosis in front of me every day
I see the ones that chose it—wild-eyed and deranged
I see 'em givin' up and givin' in and turnin' on their neighbor
Always wearin' their fake virtue all puffed up like they a savior
Others look away 'cuz they just scared to call it out
That is why it's goin' on so long 'cuz they afraid to shout
They forgot that they human or think they are superior
Talk out both sides of they mouth, don't believe the exterior
Guess with blinders on they stayin' super busy playin' God
Easy for 'em to believe they own made-up dialogue

But as a hail mary I will give it one more shot
As I pass 'em on the sidelines they sit shivering and lost
Snap out of it come on wake up it's OK you were wrong
You're destroying your whole life by lettin' this whole thing go on
The clown show has expired now stop hidin' your face
The absurdity must end time to rejoin the human race

Faces
I don't wanna see you lie—don't wanna see you hide your
faces
You are feeding the divide—clearly by design
Faces
I don't wanna see you lie—don't wanna see you hide your
faces
You are feeding the divide—clearly by design

I see 'em hide behind all kinda of special disguises
Hypnosis-driven anxiety-ridden always self-righteous
They dying to be special wear a thousand made-up labels
Makin' self-created problems wastin' energy on fables
Twistin' facts to fit agendas, use theatrics, shape the lies
But 2 + 2 is 4 not 5 no matter how they shout or cry
They fan the flames of tribal war to set themselves apart
Long as they can keep a distance they don't see your heart
Attention seeking is their meaning livin' for the mob
Othering and playing victim is their full-time job
The face a unique signature I wanna see your souls
No time for foolish tricks and games of clickbait radicals

I wanna see your real self, not your fabrication
If you don't know who that is it can take time to awaken
Believin' the deception will give you no advantage
One day you'll have to face yourself and realize the damage.

Faces
I don't wanna see you lie—don't wanna see you hide your
faces
You are feeding the divide—clearly by design
Faces
I don't wanna see you lie—don't wanna see you hide your
faces
You are feeding the divide—clearly by design

I just wanna see your faces
No more blindness mindless stasis.

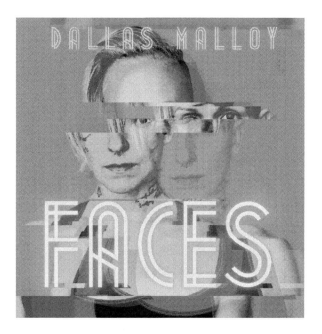

I shot music videos for "Terrible," "Slaves & Criminals," and "Will You Stand Up?" on my seven-year-old iPhone in and around my tiny studio apartment. I composed and recorded the piano music on my portable keyboard, then—wedged in a closet not wide enough to stand in straight—recorded the vocals on my voiceover mic. But where the recording space fell short, passion filled in the blanks. These were expressions of war, and the power that emerges from it. We either rise up above this, or we are swallowed up by it to languish in denial and defeat. Witnessing both, as grueling as it can be, rising up is the one and only option. I'm grateful for this awareness and strength that comes only from intense training in the wilderness.

Dear God, I am a blank canvas for You to paint what You want. Draw what You Will. I am fresh manuscript paper for You to compose what You desire. I await Your lyrics, Your notes, Your melodies, Your ideas, Your direction, Your ways, more You, less me.

And remember, never argue with crazy.

You can't rationalize with the irrational. So when they accuse you of slapping them in the face while they passive-aggressively beat you into the ground,

when they call you racist while they make your life strategically worse because of the color of *your* skin,

when they call you intolerant while silencing your online presence,

when they degrade your accomplishments and claim you need their help,

when they label you a *bigot* for not conforming to their cult, when they see you as nothing but a potential pawn for their cause,

when they judge your worth based on perceived group identity and what that means to them,

when they treat you as inhuman, worthless, without heart or soul . . . **you've already won**.

Truth needs no defense, but it inflames those who hate it. Let them be inflamed. While they melt down and continue to devalue the term *triggered* because of their made-up problems, remember you are more than a conqueror. You have the most powerful weapons available in the sword of the spirit. If that weren't true, they wouldn't fear it so much. **And they should**.

Since we have gifts that differ according to the grace given to us, each of us is to use them accordingly . . .

—from Romans 12:6

Yet in all these things we are more than conquerors and gain an overwhelming victory through Him who loved us [so much that He died for us].

—Romans 8:37

So stand firm and hold your ground, HAVING TIGHTENED THE WIDE BAND OF TRUTH (personal integrity, moral courage) AROUND YOUR WAIST AND HAVING PUT ON THE BREASTPLATE OF RIGHTEOUSNESS (an upright heart), and having strapped on YOUR FEET THE GOSPEL OF PEACE IN PREPARATION [to face the enemy with firm-footed stability and the readiness produced by the good news].
Above all, lift up the [protective] shield of faith with which you can extinguish all the flaming arrows of the evil one.
And take THE HELMET OF SALVATION, and the sword of the Spirit, which is the Word of God.

—Ephesians 6:14–17

PART 5

REFUSE NOT TO SHINE

*A*re you an anchor or a light?

Everything in this world system is designed to bring down and darken. Use you, abuse you, make you live to consume, and discard you into the human scrapheap after sucking you dry. I don't think it's possible to return to the innocence of childhood, but once you've been nearly crushed, a greater joy can be revealed.

It is not about *thinking positive* and denying this realm can be a drag and at times an unbearable struggle. The decision to be an anchor or a light in each unfolding moment determines if we hide or shine. It's possible to go through grief and still be a light, not a bliss ninny with your head in the sand, but at peace, rising above the stupid, silly repetitiousness of this world.

I got to a place where I couldn't stand living beneath my ability. And in order to advance to the levels I knew God had in store for me, I had to become more receptive to deeper spiritual work and training. I've made this my focal point. And practice living above my circumstances.

Are you living beneath your ability?

Mentally?
Physically?
Spiritually?
Emotionally?
Intellectually?
Financially?

Are you afraid to bring light into a room?

When I was in the downward spiral of bulimia, my lying mind told me—*convinced* me—I couldn't be at peace or be happy, unless I looked a certain way. And that way was always out of reach. No matter how muscular and ripped, it was *never good enough* but for a few unsustainable moments. I thought I couldn't accept a compliment or relax.

One of the cruelties of eating disorders and other addictions is the circulating lies that—short of spiritual intervention—dominate freely.

Hey, loser—it's never good enough!
Love, Bulimia

I used to let negative self-talk flow without restraint until I was drowning in self-contempt. When my life was being reshaped, I learned to start catching it. Definitely one of the harder habits to break. I eventually developed a practice where if the destructive self-talk started to chatter, I would immediately say—aloud if possible—"**You know that's a lie.**" I did this as many times as necessary. But as I did more spiritual work, the necessity soon became rare. Sometimes, trying to break a habit, people get discouraged; they fall back into doing what they've always done, but *that's the key time*—to just keep applying tools like this again and again and again. Although possible, rarely does a change stick on the first try. Persistence is the answer.

After stating **you know that's a lie**, follow it immediately with the opposite to create a *new habit*—something great and positive like:

I'm victorious!

I'm improving daily on all levels and worthy of respect and love.

If you hear *any* negative self-directed words, start employing this technique until you don't have to. Stay attuned to your inner dialogue and practice catching the trash talk such as:

I'm a loser, I mess up everything.

I'm never going to . . .

This always happens . . .

Say:

You know that's a lie. I'm victorious. I'm being rebuilt better and stronger. Everything I lay my hand to prospers and succeeds!

After a long stretch, when I was gratefully free from bulimia—and negative self-talk as well—that critical voice snuck in one day. I did some insignificant human thing, like spilling a glass of something, and in my head I heard: *idiot.* Even before I struck it down, I heard another voice quietly respond: *how dare you.* I agreed; I've conquered this enemy—I tell it: **You have no power here. I'm victorious and at peace.**

Always persistently run toward the giants. They will always be diminished while you stand victorious for facing them and refusing to bow down to shadows and trickery. Always persevere.

I have glimpsed one of my child photos and thought: *How can you possibly say such brutal things to that kid?* The adult world makes it easy to shut down that tenderness toward who we are. But no matter how hideous of a state one can deteriorate into, there was innocence once.

I live for God, and I know that separates me. But I can't live for the mundane world that hates God. I love the *natural* world, the earth and creatures, the people (not all our actions), and God-inspired creativity. Not the *world system* of greed and enslavement. Living for God is *exciting;* difficult, but *miraculous.* It is *freedom* from the world while still being productive in it; to be salt and light. To be *in it but not of it.*

Be encouraged.

I used to hear: "*Someone is praying for you*" and bitterly roll my eyes. Self-pity struck it as untrue or just worthless. All lies. There are many who pray for all living beings throughout the earth. If you're alive, that means you. *You are loved. You are unique. You are fearfully and wonderfully made.*

Prayer is one of the greatest tools at our disposal. Like any weapon it must be utilized to work. Anyone who prays consistently knows how awesomely effective it is. Lamenting the wretched state of the world as a reason not to pray is walking away from a war you are capable of winning—playing right into the hand of the forces working to keep you separate from God.

When I got sober I learned to help others in order to help myself—starting as a life-saving necessity; selfish, but productive.

Then it became: I help others because I *want* to.

Then it became: I help others because I *have* to; I *can't help it.*

And then: I help because I *get* to, to serve God.

Every day is a walk down the line between good and evil, making a choice in each unfolding moment. If we don't consciously choose, it chooses us. We all know which one wins if we keep our eyes closed. Spiritual warfare is always raging, but the wicked cannot bring down the strong with intimidation if you really know your strength and authority.

Stop apologizing for your quality.

I used to downplay my talents and abilities to coddle fragile egos around me. I put an end to that. I'd rather be alone and respect myself than live in self-degradation—and inevitable self-loathing. I've lived there before. It sucks.

Will you be fearless?

Will you refuse to be bullied and pressured into agreed-upon lies?

Will you trust God over the world system?

Are you an anchor or a light?

At work, at home, in traffic?

I've trained over fifteen hundred people. Through countless sessions and classes I've coached while going through heartbreak, divorce, loss of loved ones, depression, suicidal ideation, grief, and not knowing if I'd be able to pay rent. Sometimes I missed the mark, but I learned to receive God's help in *shifting my mindset* to focus sincerely on the people in front of me and what they need so I can deliver my best.

For the record, I never thought I wanted any of these lessons. But as I learned in boxing, you just have to **suck it up**. I can see how it would be tempting to stay in grief and be the martyr or victim the culture worships, but that's a trap—and drains all potential power from your being. The higher lessons come from walking *through*, not staying down. As I've seen God's grace transform devastating things into miracles more times than I can count, it would be a horrible disservice to pretend anyone is stuck where they are.

Remember love?

The world system is designed to suffocate love and enthusiasm, to keep you down. Like the factory workers in the 1927 formidable, expressionist, classic silent film *Metropolis*, shoulders slumped, heads down, moving in mindless unison to their soul-crushing jobs.

During the idiotic lockdowns, I had a vision of a small-business owner in a warm, vividly depicted shop. She was standing with open arms and a smile on her face, excited to serve people with her products and service. An obviously hard worker, she was striving to welcome her customers and serve them with joy. *Love drove her.* But she was shut down and told NO. A symbol of the face of the best of humanity—resilient, industrious, creative, with a heart to serve. I felt the deep ache and rage of every small-business owner and entrepreneur like me. I will always stand in righteous indignation with the brave who did not comply.

This is what they attempted to extinguish in cruel and calculated stay-at-home orders. Who? The establishment pulling the strings. Those who pushed this down on the people. Those running the farce, propping up the narrative, and punishing those who didn't go along. Remember the coercion? The manipulation? The public shaming? Nonsensical and arbitrary measures like standing six feet apart. "Vaccine" mandates—could it be more Orwellian? Euphemisms like "social distancing." I watched the survival rate percentage consistently staying in the high nineties. The *survival* rate. The data never matched the narrative.

Maybe you say it was miscalculations. And maybe some meant well. But the consistency of orchestrated efforts coming from the political talking heads, fake news media, and big tech (but I repeat myself) were (are) one voice. Have you noticed? If you didn't follow the narrative, you risked having your social media throttled. *The thought police.* Somehow it's never for your benefit. Hmm. We went through the greatest wealth transfer of our lifetime. You feel it? How many so-called "conspiracy theories" from 2020 that would get you canceled online were quietly accepted as true a year or two later? Where's the back pay for demonetized political opponents—for those conservative platforms that were shut down online? Hoping we'll forget. No chance. Where are the public apologies? Where are the firings of those who "went along"? Oh, but it was all with your best interests in mind though, right? No, it never is. Surely the wisest thing for overall health is to steal your livelihood and shut down gyms and churches. But don't worry. Liquor stores and strip clubs were good to go for the most part.

Rules for thee but not for me.

You don't live in a free country when the laws aren't applied equally. Let me count the ways . . . The war on information is a serious threat. The manipulation and suppression continues now, see it? Feel the tension? The entire DNC and the media entertainment industrial establishment work in tandem to control, suppress, demonetize, shadow ban and silence dissenting voices. This isn't a theory— they talk about it openly. Ever-changing *"Community Guidelines"* online applying to one and not another, and by design too vague to understand. And of course there's no accountability. Your livelihood can just be smashed in a day because a few people in power positions don't like words you say. Label opposing views as "hate speech,"— that ever-expanding term. Get your account suspended. Steal your livelihood. How is demonetization different from breaking into your business and stealing your profit—*and all of your future profit?* But instead of holding you at gunpoint it's done by a few people sitting behind computer screens. Algorithms designed to amplify one and suppress another—and always going in one direction. Hmm. It's almost as if the people have one specific world view they're pushing. Oh and they hate you.

Imagine if this regime had the unfettered power they desperately crave. As it is, we are witnessing the daily abuse and flagrant defiance of the Constitution: jailing political opponents, holding protesters who committed no crimes in prison for *years*, while others are given free reign to riot, loot, destroy property, and take over city blocks—without any real consequence. It's not about the crime; it's about *who* is committing it.

Face it, the so-called leaders are failing—refusing?—to protect American citizens, letting violent criminals in the country illegally, and continually working hard to erode our second Amendment rights and ability to defend ourselves. They have blood on their hands. Gee, it's as though they want us to die in filth and poverty. Haven't you had enough?

I think this goes beyond any political party. Hasn't it become apparent we're facing spiritual warfare? Look how long the concerted effort to push secular religion and remove God from every aspect of society has been going on. Look how well it's working. See the results. Do you see the anti-God—particularly anti-Christian—and anti-human sentiments that have saturated our culture? The coordinated assault from every angle on the nuclear family? The aggressive anti-Americanism? Do you see how all the major institutions have been infiltrated with this hatred? The pointed attack on the largest portion of the population?

Great Awakening

But within this crumbling nation, there is a great awakening happening that *cannot be stopped.* And it's not only here.

Hearts are coming alive worldwide. Feel it? Resistance is growing. You will never see this covered on legacy media. But truth has a way of always coming out. Never despair. Resist and stand firm.

The God spark can't be tamed or taken if we don't relinquish it. I think the globalists simultaneously disbelieve and fear that, fostering a split mind that fuels hatred for God and humanity, making it easy to want to wreck and remake. It doesn't matter, because emerging from all the shock and grieving has come a massive refueling of *determination* and resurgence of hope. God-realization is pouring out into the hearts of those willing, infusing them with power and unshakable calm. Eyes are opening. Minds are focusing.

One of the beautiful things that comes from the ashes of grief is a stripping away of superficiality. No energy is wasted. I can't be mean. I can't be mad. Only God-directed deliberate action will do.

I've observed countless times while coaching how people tend to underestimate their strength and ability to endure and overcome. I think we just don't *want* to endure, by nature, but since resistance creates more pain, that survival mechanism to avoid and conserve has to be managed— and often overridden.

At sixteen, when I stepped into the ring for the history-making match, in my mind it was already done—I'd already won. In spite of the many arrows in my back, the intense work, preparation, and focus of the mission pulled me through to completion. My vision is always bigger than me, but I didn't know God yet. So, after the inspiration waned,

I fell into oblivion with no foundation to manage the tidal wave pulling me to extremes.

The ongoing task of navigating and cultivating a balanced and inspired life has evolved more into an art than a chore. The speck of willingness I found while strung out in a treatment center lit the halls of hope for a new existence— treacherous but *covered*. Still in the valley of the shadow of death, but this time I was walking *through*, not gazing at the darkness—mistaking it for life and staying there to rot, as the extraordinary existence that could have been vanished in smoke.

Don't you think it's your time to decide *never again* to live beneath your ability; to stand up and fight? See your future self looking back with respect at what you did today. Time to abandon living for the world and being a slave to the world system. Pick up the sword of the spirit and use it. We have to go into battle, knowing we've already won; and fighting the good fight of faith *is* a fight we win. We have to *run* into battle. The light of God is placed in everyone, but it doesn't impose. We can ignore it at will, but it remains, eternally patient. It is the fragrance that exquisitely transforms everything it lives and moves through—when invited. Humbly seeking is the glorious key that allows it to shine freely, and *so will you*.

*But those who wait for the Lord
[who expect, look for, and hope in Him]
Will gain new strength and renew their power;
They will lift up their wings [and rise up close to
God] like eagles [rising toward the sun];
They will run and not become weary,
They will walk and not grow tired.*

—Isaiah 40:31

*Be strong and courageous, do not be afraid or tremble
in dread before them, for it is the LORD your God who
goes with you. He will not fail you or abandon you.*

—Deuteronomy 31:6

*Let us not grow weary or become discouraged in
doing good, for at the proper time we will reap,
if we do not give in.*

—Galatians 6:9

*Even though I walk through the [sunless]
valley of the shadow of death,
I fear no evil, for You are with me;
Your rod [to protect] and Your staff [to guide],
they comfort and console me.*

—Psalm 23:4

I will give thanks and praise to You, for I am
fearfully and wonderfully made;
Wonderful are Your works,
And my soul knows it very well.

—*Psalm 139:14*

Not that I speak from [any personal] need,
for I have learned to be content [and self-sufficient
through Christ, satisfied to the point where
I am not disturbed or uneasy] regardless of
my circumstances.

Philippians 4:11

I have given to them Your word [the message You
gave Me]; and the world has hated them because they
are not of the world and do not belong to the world,
just as I am not of the world and do not belong to it.

—*John 17:14*

You are the salt of the earth . . .
You are the light of [Christ to] the world . . .

—*from Matthew 5:13-14*

But thanks be to God, who always leads us in triumph in Christ, and through us spreads and makes evident everywhere the sweet fragrance of the knowledge of Him.

—2 Corinthians 2:14

Fight the good fight of the faith [in the conflict with evil]; take hold of the eternal life to which you were called, and [for which] you made the good confession [of faith] in the presence of many witnesses.

—1 Timothy 6:12

. . . David ran quickly toward the battle line to meet the Philistine.

—from 1 Samuel 17:48

PART 6

THIS IS NOT OVER

Within days of what I thought was the completion of this book, USA Boxing, which governs amateur boxing—the entity I sued as a sixteen-year-old for the right to box—announced they would be allowing biological males to "compete" against women. So here we go again. But this time the battle is stranger and darker.

If I still possessed the ability to be shocked by anything, this would qualify. If I were boxing now, I would refuse to fight until they did the right thing. Of course, I'll wager that allowing biological males (why am I saying "biological"? They're males, the end) to "compete" against women is occurring for political reasons, as per the usual agreement. I wonder what kind of money changed hands. Just saying. I wonder how many more might pay to watch such a bloodbath? Guaranteed to attract a desirable crowd and best for all involved. Well done. This is not, nor has it ever been, about *compassion* or *inclusion*. By now, those words have taken such a beating they are nearly unrecognizable. In any case, this dumpster fire of a decision is clearly the business of wrecking ambitions and breaking spirits. We know this goes far beyond boxing, but were it boxing alone, that would be bad enough.

I will always defend the sanctity of the sport. I love it. I had to fight just to get in the ring. And the currently registered female boxers are there in part because of the pioneering work I did; I say this in all humility. I opened the door for them. They now have the opportunity to take their own stands. Their biggest fight may also be outside the ring, but this time by refusing to get in it as long as this sinister ruling rests on the books. This is their time to truly show what it means to be a fighter, and I pray they do. The same goes for any eager supporters, fans, followers, and contributors to USA Boxing: cut off the support, dry up the money, and we stop the bleeding. On a dime.

Sometimes the battles we face are not what we expected. Sometimes they cause us to lose friends and family. Sometimes the people we thought would stand by our side until the end are the ones who turn their backs first. But that doesn't make it wrong to fight when you know you are on the side of what is right. It's time to wake up and pay attention to what's happening. We won't let men be erased. We won't let women be erased. Biology is real—facts are facts.

I never made my battle to get in the ring a women's-rights issue. I was pursuing a dream and was discriminated against. The policy was wrong; so I fought it and won. But now, it's impossible not to see the serious threat to women and girls—in this attack on them. Punished for their biology. As of the moment I write this, the rule states the boxers have to be over eighteen, having undergone sex-reassignment surgery and have had four years of hormone therapy. *Over eighteen.* That means more than likely they went through male puberty or at least partially, meaning they are men. No amount of hormones or surgeries can ever entirely undo the biological reality of bone structure, muscle mass, lung capacity, speed, and size. When a male MMA fighter who identifies as trans reportedly broke two of his female opponent's skulls, he was called the bravest athlete in history. Such over-the-top praise shows the extreme effort to gaslight people and force down antiscientific ideas. Men and women are different. *I just can't believe I have to say this.*

I slap my forehead, saying, "Is this really necessary"? Yes, it is. Take a man and a woman at *the exact same weight.* Who's stronger? No contest. The male. However, who's the better fighter? There, you can't answer. You can't know just by the weight. Nevertheless, if a 195-pound male slams his fist into a 195-pound female and vice versa, the effect is far different. It's no contest; I've coached men and women at multiple skill levels. The best male will always beat the best female. Entertaining fantasies has been a massive distraction and appalling waste of time. But that's the purpose, right? It's hard to fathom anything more anti-woman. Of course there are extremely rare exceptions. But functional systems aren't based on anomalies.

I've never dwelled on the unique brand of discrimination I've encountered as a female athlete, but it is a definite thing. Besides facing down USA Boxing and succeeding in my fight for them to establish a women's division (the one they're now working to destroy, LOL), I've experienced countless subtle digs, jokes at my expense, and bizarre hypercriticism. Sometimes interviewers would try to make it "cute"—like in articles, calling me a "*girl* boxer." You're assumed to be a bitch, a bully, be of low intelligence or have mental issues. But by all means, at the same time you have to measure up to a man. In any case, you're not taken seriously. Also, you better not show any vulnerability. None of it makes sense. At seventeen I left an abusive boyfriend on the West Coast in Washington and had a police escort when I was moving out. As I recounted that dreadful scene, someone said, "Aren't you a boxer? Couldn't you just have fought him off?" *Oh yeah, of course. Why didn't I think of that? I'll just fight him off with one hand and move my piano with the other. Perfect.*

It is difficult for me to comprehend that level of ignorance. I'm sure attitudes like that would go for athletes in general, and certainly as a female athlete, you must be indestructible, inhuman, without emotion or weak points. Psychological abuse can chip away at *anyone*, including men, regardless of career, perceived authority, or status. Two things can be true at once; it's possible to be strong and disciplined in one area and lacking in self-worth and tools in another. Sometimes female police officers find themselves in abusive relationships. I've known men who were badly abused by women. I have deep compassion for them—in particular as they face the added burden of societal shame and pressure to keep it quiet.

Athletes are often shoved into the one-dimensional category. Particularly when I was competing in bodybuilding, because that kind of physical extreme stands out, I frequently got comments from guys like: *"So you could probably beat me up, right?"* Anytime I met someone new, the first thing out of their mouth was usually a joke. My physique had to be put into either a threat category or a worship category. Some would say I asked for it, but that would be based on the assumption my bodybuilding had anything to do with other people, which it did not. My appearance had to be a topic; I couldn't just *be*.

One time a waiter I often chatted with at a restaurant gave me this screwy look when I went to pay and handed him my credit card that happened to have a kitten photo theme. How did it come about that someone with an unusually muscular physique also adored soft, fuzzy little creatures? He couldn't wrap his mind around it. I get it—it's a shallow reaction. But seriously, *how dense*. And for the record, I could easily write a book about my insatiable love for cats and kittens, so deal with it. (Dogs too).

By the way, I don't recall ever being told I was *brave and beautiful,* the phrase the establishment currently reserves for an athlete—or anyone, really—who rejects their gender. The bar couldn't be lower here in clown world. To be clear: I don't *need* to be told. The salient point is: this is a silly place. Just another confirmation in my overflowing cup— why I don't live for the world.

No one can accurately judge, emulate, or steal the unique experiences we have, not just as athletes, but as females. I don't need understanding or even empathy, but an attempt to minimize and erase any relevance of personal life experiences is not acceptable and will not be tolerated.

And it goes even deeper. *Every* living thing endures hardship in this world, and the last time I checked, there was no one inside this skin with me. I loathe the common practice of comparing brands of suffering; being incalculable, it is futile and divisive. Shine the light on this wretched attempt to undermine us all. This sleight of hand will not work. We see the tricks and they are very dirty.

I know that boxing, bodybuilding, and artistic endeavors are not for everyone. But they have all been for me. The freedom to pursue what I am drawn to is one that I prize highly. *This* is the lesson—*permission?*—that anyone can adopt.

There are risks a boxer takes, as with any athletic pursuit—particularly the fighting sports—but it's a calculated risk when you are placed in *fair* competition with the same gender. No two people are identical, but separating by gender is as fair as it gets.

Few people want to become athletes; a small number actually *become* them. A smaller portion of those are boxers, and a minority are female. Pretending large swathes of the male population are suddenly lining up to become female (as if that were *actually* possible) and *that they also dream of becoming a boxer* is the dumbest sell I've heard—and that's after enduring the covidiocracy of 2020. This goes for all women's sports currently being denigrated by a steady stream of attacks. The loud push is to get us to believe the numbers are so great they rival the number of female athletes, but more accurately, *they supersede their importance.* No one has to say it—it's obvious. Look where all the attention is going. It is easy to see there is a manufactured social contagion to reject your gender. Nicely done, TikTok. The fact that it is occurring predominantly in specific locations—larger metropolitan cities—is just one of the many clues.

I must also mention how astonishingly insulting it is to those of us who push the edge of the envelope as female athletes—always going beyond the norm to test and challenge ourselves. This phony "inclusiveness" completely dilutes that and devalues—to the point of evaporation—record-breaking achievements, which disappear into some memory fading into the background. But that's the idea, see? It will never work if we don't let them get away with it.

Fun fact: *"inclusiveness"* now means only *a select few*. The manipulation of language is one of the main tactics of the radical left. Soft words and euphemisms are easy to hear and overlook. They tickle the ears while hijacking the meaning, hoping you won't notice. *"Diversity"* means anti-White unless, being White, you still think identically with them (but you're still less valuable—don't forget!) Simply: it's not *ever* what they claim. This may be the one way in which they are consistent.

Question: why aren't there large numbers of females who call themselves males competing in men's sports? Why are they not breaking records there if it's all the same? We know why, but let us all keep pretending. Solid plan.

I'm not going to feed the narcissism machine and put my attention where the establishment of lies is trying to socially engineer it to go. I'm not going to ignore the safety and well-being of the majority to accommodate a few feelings or out of fear of offending. The request to do so is insulting. Of course, it doesn't come as a request, but as a *demand*—or you risk the wrath of the woke mob. But the *awake* don't fear any man—sorry, I mean any *twerp*.

If you want to talk about *offensive*, we can start with the egregious insult to our intelligence, the assault on our personal experiences and struggles, and the attempt to minimize and finally eliminate men and women. *That* is offensive.

To be crystal clear, I'm referring to "woke" as the current definition, meaning someone who believes in intersectionality, political correctness, micro-aggressions, endless genders, having your own pronouns. Leftists. Someone who believes there are *systemic* injustices built into our society. *Systemic* being the keyword here. "Woke mob" refers to self-proclaimed (and many paid) activists who take the most radical position with these ideologies and make it their job to shut down (silence, cancel, maybe even dox, harass, or worse) those who don't go along. If promoting sex changes for minors and pornography in their schools isn't demonic, I don't know what is. Yes these things are really happening, along with infecting all major institutions with DEI. This stands for Diversity, Equity, and Inclusion, but more accurately: anti-White, guaranteed outcome regardless of merit, and exclusion of those who don't have the same worldview.

I know the term "gaslighting" gets overused, but it seems to be the favorite tactic of this radical movement; relentlessly accusing you of doing what *they're* doing, trying to manipulate you into feeling guilty, confused about reality—and invalid.

True justice is a good thing. But the current state of lawlessness in major cities, horrendous liberal policies that favor criminals over legitimate victims, wide open borders, and other examples of radical progressive (*transgressive*) ideas show the absolute failure of wokeism. It is unjust in every way; only a tool for manipulating endless power and control. Simply, evil.

Side note: this is the opportunity to shed people-pleasing once and for all if you contend with this particular defect. The remnants of it were painfully—thankfully—ripped from me in the last few years. I acknowledge the fact that this agenda is wicked and the people pushing it don't care about you or me. Good. I don't need their care, understanding, or empathy. Their coddling of feelings only goes in one direction. Don't need it or want it. Just saying. There is more than enough love, power, genuine selfless support, affection and encouragement among *us*, the sane remainder, who have eyes open and sound minds in check. And make no mistake, the majority of people are not buying any of this, but they are not all brave enough to stand up and say it, feeding into the illusion created by the establishment media that this is all normal and accepted. That's a hard NO. Remember, God knows your struggle. And your gut was always right to not buy what they're selling. Carry on. And keep speaking up loud and clear for all to hear.

The logical solution for USA Boxing and other athletic organizations would be to create a separate division. So why isn't that being done (as of the moment I write this)? When I wanted to box, I fought for a women's division to be created. I didn't demand to be in the men's division and insist they accommodate me by, I don't know, not hitting as hard? Of course that would have been asinine, but no less than the current situation. Evidently, the decision-makers are not interested in solutions. It is plain to see this push is leapfrogging over them, with the effect of disrupting, deceiving, taking down, and eliminating. It's like a sickness got into their brains, and they can't fight it off. That's what ideas can do.

Bad enough.

It's too easy for someone to look away and think: *It doesn't concern me. Who cares about women's sports?* Fine, but when will it be bad enough? Whether people accept the fact or not, the physical advantages males have over females are *widely known and unquestionable.* Do women have to get killed in the ring? And why does it have to go to that extreme to prove a point? Cheating women and girls out of the thrill of victory and the confidence that goes with it should be bad enough. Cheating them out of fair competition and the priceless lessons that come from it should be bad enough. Stealing livelihoods and opportunities should be bad enough. Ruining their sports career should be bad enough. Stealing their sense of accomplishment and hard-earned achievement should be bad enough. Cheating them out of the basic fun of sports and fair play should be bad enough. Violating their basic right to privacy and safety in locker rooms and bathrooms should be bad enough. I could easily go on, but it turns my stomach.

So I just want to know if you're going to stand with me, and stop allowing yourself to be bullied and gaslit by cowardice, and never again go along with the agreed-upon lies. When these narratives of deception come up online, in the lamestream media, in conversation, wherever, will you speak up? I'm not talking about pointless online fighting with trolls. I mean speaking up when it counts, when it matters: when you are maliciously accused of falsities—such as being called a bigot for not buying into the cult—will you determine that's the end of that conversation, knowing the truth needs no defense? Only the guilty have to explain themselves. Will you state facts and step away from the unhinged? Will you call out the corruption? Will you guard your heart and mind for what really matters in life and not trade it to battle with the foolish and/or mentally ill? Will you calmly stand strong and not let any of it interfere with your precious peace? Will you be unmoved? Will you spend your hard-earned money on products from companies that support your values or at least don't work toward your demise? You are already voting with your dollars—but doing it intentionally makes a dent and sends the message—*we are done with this.* "*Go woke go broke*" isn't just a cute saying. It *is* cute, though, in addition to being true.

When I got sober, I was warned about drowning in overthinking and excessive complexity. To save my life, I was told to keep it simple, and most of all: you have to decide, God either *is* or He *isn't.* What'll it be? No matter how limited my understanding of God was at the time, it would suffice, as long as I knew it wasn't *me.* And that I couldn't *think* my way into a spiritual awakening. In a sense, my circumstances tossed me into one by reducing my options so rapidly there was nothing left to do but accept it willingly. The gift of desperation; gold wrapped in ashes and soot. Then I was open to going deeper, continuing to seek in this realm that was new to me, and receive revelation down in my being.

Winning in spiritual warfare.

There was a point recently where I got fed up with giving into worry, anxiety, and doubt. These devilish little irritants accomplish nothing good and are the antithesis of living a life of faith. Indulging them at all is a form of addiction and pride; telling God I don't trust Him, I don't need help, and I can fix it if I just think about it enough. *A wretched habit that needed serious undoing.* I felt that firm knowing and decision. These words rose up in me and I've been declaring them loudly since then anytime worry or any negative thing tries to invade, and even better—*before* it has a chance:

Worry is a tool of the enemy and it is bound and crushed beneath my feet.

Anxiety is a tool of the enemy and it is bound and crushed beneath my feet.

Doubt is a tool of the enemy and it is bound and crushed beneath my feet.

This is all in the name of Jesus Christ.

I have learned to practice walking by faith, not by sight. That used to make my rational mind squirm, but now it's calmed by this knowledge. Because it works. And no war of deception inside or out will keep me from that fact.

Please reach for God. Take spiritual authority and don't look back. And when the doubt comes in, you know what to do. Pray and receive His marching orders that are always for your good.

So when things are shaking, when it looks like everything is falling apart, when things seem to be getting worse, not better—we know it's usually darkest before the dawn—will you keep your eye on God and know you're part of something bigger, something greater? Will you not be distracted by political theater and visual tricks? Will you trust Him and say it aloud, and trust His promise to work all things for good for those who love Him? I prayed: I trust you God—for a long time before I felt it. It's not a feeling. It's a decision.

Child of God, will you use the sword of the spirit and live it? Will you stand and face whatever is necessary, knowing you are more than a conqueror? Will you keep your eyes on God and follow His Direction no matter what? Patriot, will you stand up and fight?

Am I now trying to win the favor and approval of men, or of God? Or am I seeking to please someone? If I were still trying to be popular with men, I would not be a bond-servant of Christ.

—Galatians 1:10

The LORD is on my side; I will not fear. What can [mere] man do to me?

—Psalm 118:6

For we walk by faith, not by sight [living our lives in a manner consistent with our confident belief in God's promises]

—2 Corinthians 5:7

So submit to [the authority of] God. Resist the devil [stand firm against him] and he will flee from you.

—James 4:7

"No weapon that is formed against you will succeed;
And every tongue that rises against you in judgment
you will condemn.
This [peace, righteousness, security, and triumph over opposition] is the heritage of the servants of the LORD,
And this is their vindication from Me," says the LORD.

—Isaiah 54:17

PART 7

COMBAT TOOLS FOR SPIRITUAL WARFARE

The necessity to wake up to spiritual warfare has never been more apparent and grows by the minute. Days of sitting on the sidelines are finished. There is no time for apathy. Playing neutral is assisting the adversary.

Here are all the aforementioned tools, affirmations, prayers, and Scripture in full—they are great weapons laid at your feet to help you stand up and fight. No matter how deep in the wilderness you find yourself, you will come out of it **victorious** if you take spiritual authority and **never give up.** Fighting the good fight of faith is a fight we win.

Death and life are in the power of the tongue—with every word we are creating or tearing down. Sometimes you have to act and talk your way into right thinking; then the feelings will follow.

To help you end procrastination and build self-respect and confidence:

> *Do the dreaded task first.*

To help you stop smoking—SAY:

> *This will definitely pass, and I don't want to be a smoker forever, so if I just don't light up, I will never have to go through THIS again.*

To help you find purpose and combat self-pity—PRAY:

> *Show me who I can help today. Show me what You want me to do today.*

Challenge:

> *Help someone without being found out and without telling anyone. No selfies . . . no posting . . .*

To help you stop negative self-talk—talk back to the enemy:

You know that's a lie.

I've been expecting you to show up, and you're not going to get me this time.

You've already taken enough of my life, and you're not getting any more of it.

You are dismissed.

You have no power here.

I rebuke you in the name of Jesus Christ.

Create a new habit and follow it up with an affirmation:

I am victorious!

I only think thoughts that heal me and bless me and others.

I am improving daily on all levels and worthy of respect and love.

I am being rebuilt better and stronger.

Everything I lay my hand to prospers and succeeds!

I am victorious and at peace.

MORE AFFIRMATIONS

Anxiety is a tool of the enemy and it is bound and crushed beneath my feet.

Worry is a tool of the enemy and it is bound and crushed beneath my feet.

Doubt is a tool of the enemy and it is bound and crushed beneath my feet.

This is all in the name above every name, Jesus Christ.

I graciously and gratefully receive everything God wants me to have.

I am totally capable and can accomplish anything I set my mind to.

I can do all things through Christ Who is my strength.

I am not afraid of confrontation. I love confrontation because it's a game. And it's a game called I WIN.

The better I get at listening, the better I get at hearing, and receiving Assistance.

I'm excited! I'm excited about this opportunity to show my work and talent.

I am more than a conqueror.

I am more than enough, and I have everything I need within me to accomplish any task set before me.

I am the righteousness of God in Christ.

No weapon formed against me shall prosper.

Greater is He Who is in me than is in the world.

I am strong and courageous.

I am the head and not the tail, above and not beneath.

God is my strength and my shield.

With God all things are possible.

With God I am unshakable and unbreakable.

God is bigger than every storm, and I am being taken care of.

LIFE CLEANING

What are you living for?

How do you want to be remembered?

Who do you see when you look in the mirror?

Who do you want to see?

Do you need permission to be free?

Do you need permission to be great?

Are you a people-pleaser?

A world-pleaser?

A God-pleaser?

Are you living beneath your ability?

Mentally?

Physically?

Spiritually?

Emotionally?

Intellectually?

Financially?

God help me reach my true potential on all levels.

Is this person in your life an anchor or a light?

Is this activity an anchor or a light?

Is this job an anchor or a light?

Is this career an anchor or a light?

Is this food an anchor or a light?

Are you afraid to bring light into a room?

Do you have the courage to be a light?

Of course you do.

PRAYERS

Pray without ceasing. It is an ongoing communication of talking and listening. Being quiet. It's a practice. It works.

Lord, please give me strength to endure this time of ripping down, knowing it is all for my good. Help me through the wilderness. Let me come out victorious and free from all that has hindered me from fulfilling Your Will for me. Let my overcoming be a light and witness everywhere I go. In Jesus' name, Amen.

Lord, let me be a mouthpiece for you. Let every word be useful—more You, less me. More you, less me. Nothing wasted, nothing missing, nothing broken.

Please show me the lesson and give me the strength to endure while completing this course. Thank you!

Please give me the courage I need in every moment.

Dear God, I feel like I can't endure any longer, but I know You love me. I know You provide an infinite supply of everything I need. I know You have great things in store for me, and I will trust You through this, knowing that magnificent things will come out of it for me and others, and I will come through it better, greater, stronger, and victorious!

Decrease me, increase You.

All of You. None of me.

How I start every day:

Father God in the name of Jesus Christ,

I trust You.

Use me.

Guide me.

Thank You.

Help me.

I love You.

Thy Will be done.

SWORD OF THE SPIRIT
Scripture from the Amplified Bible

<u>FROM PART 1</u>

I shattered them so that they were not able to rise;
They fell [wounded] under my feet.
For You have encircled me with strength for the battle;
You have subdued under me those
who rose up against me.

—*Psalm 18:38–39*

My people are destroyed for lack of knowledge [of
My law, where I reveal My will].
Because you [the priestly nation]
have rejected knowledge,
I will also reject you from being My priest.
Since you have forgotten the law of your God,
I will also forget your children.

—*Hosea 4:6*

We are pressured in every way [hedged in], but not crushed; perplexed [unsure of finding a way out], but not driven to despair; hunted down and persecuted, but not deserted [to stand alone]; struck down, but never destroyed; always carrying around in the body the dying of Jesus, so that the [resurrection] life of Jesus also may be shown in our body.

—*2 Corinthians 4:8–10*

Do not, therefore, fling away your [fearless] confidence, for it has a glorious and great reward. For you have need of patient endurance [to bear up under difficult circumstances without compromising], so that when you have carried out the will of God, you may receive and enjoy to the full what is promised.

—*Hebrews 10:35-36*

FROM PART 2

Set your mind and keep focused habitually on the things above [the heavenly things], not on things that are on the earth [which have only temporal value].

—*Colossians 3:2*

And do not be conformed to this world [any longer with its superficial values and customs], but be transformed and progressively changed [as you mature spiritually] by the renewing of your mind [focusing on godly values and ethical attitudes], so that you may prove [for yourselves] what the will of God is, that which is good and acceptable and perfect [in His plan and purpose for you].

—Romans 12:2

The Light shines on in the darkness, and the darkness did not understand it or overpower it or appropriate it or absorb it [and is unreceptive to it].

—John 1:5

Put on the full armor of God [for His precepts are like the splendid armor of a heavily-armed soldier], so that you may be able to [successfully] stand up against all the schemes and the strategies and the deceits of the devil.

For our struggle is not against flesh and blood [contending only with physical opponents], but against the rulers, against the powers, against the world forces of this [present] darkness, against the spiritual forces of wickedness in the heavenly (supernatural) places.

Therefore, put on the complete armor of God, so that you will be able to [successfully] resist and stand your ground in the evil day [of danger], and having done everything [that the crisis demands], to stand firm [in your place, fully prepared, immovable, victorious].

—Ephesians 6:11-13

FROM PART 3

*And we know [with great confidence] that God
[who is deeply concerned about us] causes all
things to work together [as a plan] for good for
those who love God, to those who are called
according to His plan and purpose.*

—Romans 8:28

*But He has said to me, "My grace is sufficient for
you [My lovingkindness and My mercy are more
than enough—always available—regardless of
the situation]; for [My] power is being perfected
[and is completed and shows itself most
effectively] in [your] weakness." Therefore, I will all
the more gladly boast in my weaknesses, so that
the power of Christ [may completely enfold me
and] may dwell in me.*

—2 Corinthians 12:9

*Rejoice always and delight in your faith; be
unceasing and persistent in prayer; in every
situation [no matter what the circumstances] be
thankful and continually give thanks to God; for
this is the will of God for you in Christ Jesus.*

—1 Thessalonians 5:16-18

Do not be anxious or worried about anything, but in everything [every circumstance and situation] by prayer and petition with thanksgiving, continue to make your [specific] requests known to God.

And the peace of God [that peace which reassures the heart, that peace] which transcends all understanding, [that peace which] stands guard over your hearts and your minds in Christ Jesus [is yours].

—*Philippians 4:6-7*

For our struggle is not against flesh and blood [contending only with physical opponents], but against the rulers, against the powers, against the world forces of this [present] darkness, against the spiritual forces of wickedness in the heavenly (supernatural) places.

—*Ephesians 6:12*

Whatever you do [whatever your task may be], work from the soul [that is, put in your very best effort], as [something done] for the Lord and not for men.

—*Colossians 3:23*

FROM PART 4

*Since we have gifts that differ according to the grace
given to us, each of us is to use them accordingly: if
[someone has the gift of] prophecy, [let him speak a new
message from God to His people] in proportion to the
faith possessed; if service, in the act of serving;
or he who teaches, in the act of teaching; or he who
encourages, in the act of encouragement; he who gives,
with generosity; he who leads, with diligence; he who
shows mercy [in caring for others], with cheerfulness.*

—Romans 12:6–8

*Yet in all these things we are more than conquerors
and gain an overwhelming victory through Him
who loved us [so much that He died for us].
For I am convinced [and continue to be convinced—
beyond any doubt] that neither death, nor life, nor
angels, nor principalities, nor things present and
threatening, nor things to come, nor powers,
nor height, nor depth, nor any other created thing,
will be able to separate us from the [unlimited]
love of God, which is in Christ Jesus our Lord.*

—Romans 8:37–39

So stand firm and hold your ground, HAVING TIGHTENED THE WIDE BAND OF TRUTH (personal integrity, moral courage) AROUND YOUR WAIST AND HAVING PUT ON THE BREASTPLATE OF RIGHTEOUSNESS (an upright heart),

and having strapped on YOUR FEET THE GOSPEL OF PEACE IN PREPARATION [to face the enemy with firm-footed stability and the readiness produced by the good news].

Above all, lift up the [protective] shield of faith with which you can extinguish all the flaming arrows of the evil one.

And take THE HELMET OF SALVATION, and the sword of the Spirit, which is the Word of God.

—Ephesians 6:14–17

FROM PART 5

But those who wait for the Lord [who expect, look for, and hope in Him]

Will gain new strength and renew their power;
They will lift up their wings [and rise up close to God] like eagles [rising toward the sun];

They will run and not become weary,
They will walk and not grow tired.

—Isaiah 40:31

*Be strong and courageous, do not be afraid or
tremble in dread before them, for it is the LORD
your God who goes with you. He will not fail
you or abandon you.*

—Deuteronomy 31:6

---

*Let us not grow weary or become discouraged in
doing good, for at the proper time we will reap,
if we do not give in.*

—Galatians 6:9

---

*Even though I walk through the [sunless]
valley of the shadow of death,*

*I fear no evil, for You are with me;
Your rod [to protect] and Your staff [to guide],
they comfort and console me.*

—Psalm 23:4

---

*I will give thanks and praise to You, for I am
fearfully and wonderfully made; Wonderful are
Your works, And my soul knows it very well.*

—Psalm 139:14

---

*Not that I speak from [any personal] need, for I have
learned to be content [and self-sufficient through
Christ, satisfied to the point where I am not disturbed
or uneasy] regardless of my circumstances.*
*I know how to get along and live humbly [in
difficult times], and I also know how to enjoy
abundance and live in prosperity. In any and every
circumstance I have learned the secret [of facing
life], whether well-fed or going hungry, whether
having an abundance or being in need.*
*I can do all things [which He has called me to do]
through Him who strengthens and empowers
me [to fulfill His purpose—I am self-sufficient in
Christ's sufficiency; I am ready for anything and
equal to anything through Him who infuses me
with inner strength and confident peace.]*
—Philippians 4:11-13

---

*I have given to them Your word [the message You
gave Me]; and the world has hated them because they
are not of the world and do not belong to the world,
just as I am not of the world and do not belong to it.*
*I do not ask You to take them out of the world, but that
You keep them and protect them from the evil one.*
They are not of the world, just as I am not of the world.
*Sanctify them in the truth [set them apart for Your
purposes, make them holy]; Your word is truth.*
*Just as You commissioned and sent Me into the
world, I also have commissioned and sent them
(believers) into the world.*

*For their sake I sanctify Myself [to do Your will],
so that they also may be sanctified [set apart,
dedicated, made holy] in [Your] truth.*

*I do not pray for these alone [it is not for their
sake only that I make this request], but also for
[all] those who [will ever] believe and trust in Me
through their message,*

*that they all may be one; just as You, Father, are in
Me and I in You, that they also may be one in Us,
so that the world may believe [without any doubt]
that You sent Me.*

—John 17:14–21

---

*You are the salt of the earth; but if the salt has lost
its taste (purpose), how can it be made salty? It is
no longer good for anything, but to be thrown out
and walked on by people [when the walkways are
wet and slippery].*

*You are the light of [Christ to] the world. A city set
on a hill cannot be hidden;*

*nor does anyone light a lamp and put it under a
basket, but on a lampstand, and it gives light to all
who are in the house.*

*Let your light shine before men in such a way
that they may see your good deeds and moral
excellence, and [recognize and honor and] glorify
your Father who is in heaven.*

—Matthew 5:13–16

But thanks be to God, who always leads us in triumph in Christ, and through us spreads and makes evident everywhere the sweet fragrance of the knowledge of Him.

—2 Corinthians 2:14

Fight the good fight of the faith [in the conflict with evil]; take hold of the eternal life to which you were called, and [for which] you made the good confession [of faith] in the presence of many witnesses.

—1 Timothy 6:12

When the Philistine rose and came forward to meet David, David ran quickly toward the battle line to meet the Philistine.

David put his hand into his bag and took out a stone and slung it, and it struck the Philistine on his forehead. The stone penetrated his forehead, and he fell face down on the ground.

—1 Samuel 17:48–49

FROM PART 6

*Am I now trying to win the favor and approval
of men, or of God? Or am I seeking to please
someone? If I were still trying to be popular with
men, I would not be a bond-servant of Christ.*

—Galatians 1:10

*The LORD is on my side; I will not fear.
What can [mere] man do to me?*

—Psalm 118:6

*So then, being always filled with good courage and
confident hope, and knowing that while we are at
home in the body we are absent from the Lord— for we
walk by faith, not by sight [living our lives in a manner
consistent with our confident belief in God's promises]—
we are [as I was saying] of good courage and confident
hope, and prefer rather to be absent from the body and
to be at home with the Lord.*

*Therefore, whether we are at home [on earth] or away
from home [and with Him], it is our [constant] ambition
to be pleasing to Him.*

*For we [believers will be called to account and] must
all appear before the judgment seat of Christ, so that
each one may be repaid for what has been done in the
body, whether good or bad [that is, each will be held
responsible for his actions, purposes, goals, motives—
the use or misuse of his time, opportunities and abilities].*

—2 Corinthians 5:6–10

So submit to [the authority of] God. Resist the devil [stand firm against him] and he will flee from you.

—*James 4:7*

"No weapon that is formed against you will succeed; And every tongue that rises against you in judgment you will condemn.

This [peace, righteousness, security, and triumph over opposition] is the heritage of the servants of the LORD, And this is their vindication from Me," says the LORD.

—*Isaiah 54:17*

MORE STRENGTH AND ASSURANCE

Then Moses said to the people, "Do not be afraid! Take your stand [be firm and confident and undismayed] and see the salvation of the LORD which He will accomplish for you today; for those Egyptians whom you have seen today, you will never see again. The LORD will fight for you while you [only need to] keep silent and remain calm."

—*Exodus 14:13-14*

---

*But on that day I will separate and set apart the
land of Goshen, where My people are living, so that
no swarms of insects will be there, so that you may
know [without any doubt] and acknowledge that I,
the LORD, am in the midst of the earth. I will put a
division (distinction) between My people and your
people. By tomorrow this sign shall be in evidence.*

—*Exodus 8:22-23*

---

*He who dwells in the shelter of the Most High
Will remain secure and rest in the shadow of the
Almighty [whose power no enemy can withstand].
I will say of the LORD, "He is my refuge and my fortress,
My God, in whom I trust [with great confidence,
and on whom I rely]!"*

—*Psalm 91:1–2*

---

*Peace I leave with you; My [perfect] peace I give you;
not as the world gives do I give to you. Do not let
your heart be troubled, nor let it be afraid. [Let My
perfect peace calm you in every circumstance and
give you courage and strength for every challenge.]*

—*John 14:27*

---

*God is our refuge and strength
[mighty and impenetrable],
A very present and well-proved help in trouble.*

—*Psalm 46:1*

---

*He who believes in Me [who adheres to, trusts in,
and relies on Me], as the Scripture has said,
'From his innermost being will flow continually
rivers of living water.'*

—*John 7:38*

---

*Instead of your [former] shame you will have a
double portion;
And instead of humiliation your people will shout
for joy over their portion.
Therefore in their land they will possess double
[what they had forfeited];
Everlasting joy will be theirs.*

—*Isaiah 61:7*

---

*Such hope [in God's promises] never disappoints
us, because God's love has been abundantly
poured out within our hearts through the Holy
Spirit who was given to us.*

—*Romans 5:5*

For from days of old no one has heard,
nor has ear perceived,
Nor has the eye seen a God besides You,
Who works and acts on behalf of the one who
[gladly] waits for Him.

—*Isaiah 64:4*

And walk continually in love [that is, value one
another—practice empathy and compassion,
unselfishly seeking the best for others], just as
Christ also loved you and gave Himself up for us,
an offering and sacrifice to God [slain for you, so
that it became] a sweet fragrance.

—*Ephesians 5:2*

Listen carefully: I have given you authority [that
you now possess] to tread on serpents and
scorpions, and [the ability to exercise authority]
over all the power of the enemy (Satan); and
nothing will [in any way] harm you.

—*Luke 10:19*

Death and life are in the power of the tongue,
And those who love it and indulge it will eat its
fruit and bear the consequences of their words.

—*Proverbs 18:21*

For with God nothing [is or ever] shall be
impossible.

—*Luke 1:37*

To the weak (this can't be you):
Wake up—get up—or get out of the way.

To the strong:
Keep your eyes on God.
Keep going and never relent.
Know your authority and use it.
Hold the line.
Never surrender.
Keep standing up.
Keep fighting.
And may God bless you beyond measure.

ACKNOWLEDGMENTS

Thank you for helping me wake up, for your courage to tell the truth and unrelenting willingness to be a light in the sea of madness,
Dr. Jordan Peterson
Steven Crowder
Ben Shapiro

Thank you, brave genius, for being a shining light, spitting truth with strength, heart, humor and power,
Tom MacDonald

Thank you for greatly blessing my life with your courageous example of what it means to be an overcomer and teaching me to know my authority in Christ,
Julie Green
Joyce Meyer

Thank you for your devotion and love for our country, for your courage, passion, strength, and vision,
Mark Meckler
Convention of States

Thank you for your courage, resilience, and reminding me of hope,
Dr. Robert Malone

Thank you for your visionary work and helping to
take entertainment back,
Hollywood 4 Freedom

Thank you for standing up and being a powerful
voice and support for women and girls in sports,
Dave and Judy Brown—Stand Tall with Dave Brown

Thank you for being a lifelong champion,
trailblazer, and hero to women's boxing,
Sue TL Fox

Thank you for your patriotism, standing for God,
home, and country,
my fellow Daughters of the American Revolution

Thank you always for your love and support,
Dean, Monroe, Minnie and Mags

REFERENCES

Sources for hard copy Bibles and online reference
https://www.biblegateway.com/
https://www.lockman.org/

Footprints in the Sand by Mary Stevenson
http://footprints-inthe-sand.com/

Dr. Jordan Peterson
https://www.jordanbpeterson.com/
https://www.youtube.com/@JordanBPeterson

GQ Interview:
https://youtu.be/yZYQpge1W5s?si=Qb2G0EcESioOL9Ga

Steven Crowder
https://www.louderwithcrowder.com/

Ben Shapiro
https://www.dailywire.com/show/the-ben-shapiro-show

Tom MacDonald
https://www.youtube.com/@TomMacDonaldOfficial

Julie Green Ministries
https://rumble.com/c/JulieGreenMinistries

Joyce Meyer
https://joycemeyer.org/

Dr. Wayne Dyer
https://www.drwaynedyer.com/

Mark Meckler
https://conventionofstates.com/news/who-is-mark-meckler-president-of-convention-of-states-action

Convention of States
https://conventionofstates.com/

Dr. Robert Malone
https://www.rwmalonemd.com/
https://rwmalonemd.substack.com/p/integrity-dignity-community

Hollywood 4 Freedom
https://www.hollywood4freedom.com/

Stand Tall with Dave Brown
https://www.standtallwithdavebrown.com/

Sue Fox
https://www.womenboxing.com/Biography.htm

Daughters of the American Revolution
https://www.dar.org/

"Heaven Beside You" - by Alice in Chains
https://youtu.be/TEAyIKJb-to?si=RY3ZU_hCeDpY4DoE

Seinfeld
"Yes! Yes! Everybody has to like me. I must be liked!"
— George Costanza, Seinfeld, Season 5: Episode 9, "The Masseuse"

ABOUT THE AUTHOR

DALLAS MALLOY, 2023 International Women's Boxing Hall of Fame Inductee, is an actor, pianist, recording artist, and coach. She is a former bodybuilding champion and portrayed herself in *Jerry Maguire*, the 1996 comedy-drama starring Tom Cruise, who narrates her true story in the opening as she boxes towards the camera. She lives with her loving husband and precious cats.

Made in the USA
Columbia, SC
09 July 2024

38209103R00083